Best of wishes -

Sincerely,

Moments
of
Devotion

Moments
of
Devotion

MEDITATIONS AND VERSE

GRACE NOLL CROWELL

New York   Nashville
ABINGDON-COKESBURY PRESS

MOMENTS OF DEVOTION

Copyright MCMLIII by Pierce & Smith

Library of Congress Catalog Card Number: 52-11308

SET UP, PRINTED, AND BOUND BY THE PARTHENON PRESS, AT NASHVILLE, TENNESSEE, UNITED STATES OF AMERICA

THIS BOOK
is affectionately dedicated to
MY FELLOW MEN

Foreword

IT IS a grave responsibility for anyone to strive to speak out to others of the things of the spirit: those intangible workings within the soul that are so difficult of expression.

In this book I have earnestly and prayerfully striven to do so, ever conscious of my own lack, but asking God's wisdom and his guidance as I worked.

If some word herein should help any journeying comrade on his way, I shall be glad, and very grateful to the One who gave me the word to say.

GRACE NOLL CROWELL

Contents

9

1

As the Day Begins

This is the day which the Lord hath made; we will rejoice and be glad in it.—Ps. 118:24

WHEN WE consider the mighty works of the Creator—the wonder of them, the splendor of them—how can we ever be unmindful of the miracle of a new day fresh from God's hands?

The dawn, with its grandeur, its portent, its opportunity to serve our Maker and our fellow men with greater wisdom and understanding than we hitherto have done, surely should be a challenge—a great and moving force in our lives.

Who could ignore the sudden startling beauty of the sun bursting above the rim of the world, the wonder of the high noon like a huge golden flower, the night with its silver splendor of stars?

Should we not stand in awe before the majesty of it all? Should we not make every effort to use the precious hours allotted us in a way that will be pleasing to our Maker? Should we not, even though sorrow darken our door or

11

pain enter in, seemingly to abide, strive to look out and beyond grief and suffering into the wonder of the new day, and know, even though we may not understand, that a mighty hand is working for the universal good and that all things are moving together for our betterment. All things, even this seeming defeat that is apparently striving to darken our sky, are working for our good. Even out beyond the grief, and beyond the suffering, good is working for us; and some day it will be revealed before our eyes, to shine there as clear as the morning and as bright as the day, if we but wait to see it.

The following incident is a lesson in sheer, glad appreciation. A little Mexican boy, living down near the Border, was called out of bed early one morning to chase his father's goats from the growing garden. It was the lad's first experience with the dawn. It came to his astonished mind like the bursting of the sun above the hills —a beauty hitherto undreamed of by him.

He gazed with rapture at the lifting silver rays; the pink and rose, spreading like a great opening flower; the golden light that ran swift-footed across the desert that lay all about him, changing its somber color to gold and crimson, to purple and mauve, until the whole world was lit with a strange glory. His beauty-loving heart was all but bursting. Had he not seen a miracle?

Later that morning he hurried to the little country schoolhouse. He ran breathlessly to tell his much-loved teacher, with the understanding heart, of his joyous experience.

"Oh, Teacher," he cried, "I saw a day begin! I saw a day begin!" and in his broken English he described the miracle he had witnessed.

Surely the great Creator looked down upon the humble child's rapture, his awareness of his gift to mankind, and was pleased. Surely he longs for all of his children to have that same sense of wonderment and appreciation over the grandeur of his creation. May we never become so leaden with sleep, so overcome with sorrow, or bewildered with suffering, that we cannot praise our Lord for the miracle of a new day with its message of hope to mankind and its sheer soul-shaking beauty that he metes out for our hearts' deep hunger. "Oh that men would praise the Lord for his goodness, for his wonderful works to the children of men!"

Living today, I forge a golden link
    That fuses with the bright chain of forever.
Lord, help me make it strong and weld it true,
    That in some far-off future it may never
Corrode or tarnish, never tear apart

To wreck the perfect whole of light and beauty.
Moment by moment, hour by precious hour,
  May I shape a link of ardent play and duty.

O master Goldsmith, view my workmanship;
  Guide thou my efforts; aid me when I falter;
Make me to know the grave importance, Lord,
  Of this brief day, my need of shrine and altar,
Where I may humbly wait and learn of thee
How best to link life to eternity.

Lord God, may we lift our eyes unto the hills
from whence cometh our help, even as did the
Psalmist of old. Our help cometh from thee
who made heaven and earth. Thou, O Lord,
hast made all things beautiful in their time. A new
day, we realize, is one of thy loveliest gifts to men.

May we walk through the hours alert to their
significance. Help us to meet the day confidently,
happily, bravely, knowing that it is thy hand that
will lead us through the hours. May we use them
for thy glory, and may we enter at last into the
new, bright, endless day of eternity, where thou
art the light forevermore. Amen.

2

Reasonable Service

I beseech you therefore, brethren, by the mercies of God, that ye present your bodies a living sacrifice, holy, acceptable unto God, which is your reasonable service.—Rom. 12:1

A CLEAN mind in a clean body, clean, strong hands with which to labor, feet ready and willing to go on errands of mercy—these are the implements given us. They should be presented to the Lord daily, a living sacrifice; and they should be used for him in just and fair-minded acts done for his glory. This, we may believe, is our reasonable service.

We are the children of one Father. We are to serve in his vineyard. We are to give ourselves and consider ourselves no more our own but the property of our Maker. This is his will and his plan for us.

He has much to say of stewardship in this business of reasonable service. We might first consider willing stewardship. The Lord, we are told, loves a cheerful giver. In the thirty-fifth chapter of Exodus, the fifth verse, we read: "Take ye from among you an offering unto the Lord: whosoever is of a willing heart." Then further on Moses says: "And every wise hearted among you shall come, and make all that the Lord hath commanded." Again he speaks of the wisehearted women whose hearts were "stirred . . . up in wisdom," and who gave of their handiwork for the furnishing of the temple.

Wisehearted men and women today are bringing their gifts to various altars. Wise, indeed, are they who cheerfully bring the first fruits of their labor to the Lord for use in furthering his kingdom. It is well to take heed to the words "wise" and "cheerful" and "willing." They are a true part of our reasonable service. Givers such as these please our Lord.

He asks so little in return for all his goodness and mercy to us. He does not require more than the tithe of one's income, but we may be sure that those who overpay on the debt they owe him will not be losers. "Bring ye all the tithes into the storehouse, . . . and prove me now herewith, saith the Lord of hosts, if I will not open you the windows of heaven, and pour you out a blessing, that there shall not be room enough to receive it." This is the word of the Lord, and he keeps his word.

He values great giving, but he also values the little service, the small coin, the cup of cold water given in his name, if these are offered cheerfully, as much as he does the great gift, the great deed.

We cannot all be "cunning workmen," the fine engraver, the skilled silversmith or goldsmith, the expert weaver; but we can give as we have been blest, and in doing so we will be bringing an acceptable gift to our Lord. May we be willinghearted, wisehearted, when it comes to reasonable service.

Too often we associate stewardship with the giving of funds alone, but there are many kinds. Take, for instance, the stewardship of time. We give our tithes, and this done, we may be inclined to go on our way, feeling that we have met our obligations; but like David of old we should cry aloud: "Remember how short my time is!" Truly it is too short with us all for mere tithing. All our time belongs to God. We recall Jesus' earnest questioning: "Wist ye not that I must be about my Father's business?"

With him there was no time to squander. There should be none for us—no time to fritter away in idleness or to spend in worse than useless pastime. We recall that Hosea spoke out in clear ringing tones to wayward Israel: "Break up your fallow ground: for it is time to seek the Lord." Truly it is time to seek him, to follow him wherever he leads. If we do so, we will be about our Father's business; and there will be no time for idle living.

We should go about doing all things as unto the Lord. We should never miss the golden opportunities of service to our kind. Time is a very precious commodity, and how we spend it counts for eternity, either one way or the other.

There is the reasonable service we render to our Lord in the stewardship of love. God showers his love upon us. Should he not find in us good soil from which the seeds of love can spring bountifully? Thus we will have much to give our fellow men by way of understanding sympathy and love, that will help ease the jolts of life and comfort, cheer, and bless them on their way.

This is a world of give and take. It is a law of life itself. We accept love from many, and we cannot dam it up in our own keeping and give nothing back. The springs would as surely dry up in the heart as they do in the desert, leaving only burning sand and bitter weeds.

He who is given much should be a great giver. He who constantly gives out love to the world about him wears a face that shines like the sun. His own pathway is lighted as well as those of others, and love is turned to him as the flowers turn to the sun.

God grant that we may take stock of ourselves in these days of world crisis—in a world that is desperately in need of brotherly love and brotherly kindness. May we be followers of our Lord and give to the limit the compassion, the sympathy, the mercy, that has been given out so freely to us.

Let us ever remember to be kind. Has not the life of Jesus taught us to be kind? Has not his love shown us a great truth, that there should be no withholding of the love that "passeth all understanding" which has been shed abroad in our hearts? His voice sounds out as clearly today as it did centuries ago: "Freely ye have received, freely give." This we know is service that the Lord will accept.

Some words are beautiful, not alone in sound,
    Nor in their few grouped letters; but there glows
Out of their meaning something man has found
    To bless him on the troubled way he goes.
Service is a word that holds the light
    Like some high beacon for our eyes to see;
Service is a selfless thing—a white
    And ever-shining luminosity.

Service for our Master, for our kind—
We note it in the home, the church, the land.
Where Christ is truly followed, there we find
    The righteous ministering with outstretched
        hand
To those in need. Oh, there is never heard
In any tongue a stronger, lovelier word!

Our Father, we would be worthy stewards in
thy sight. We would present our bodies, our lives,
our all, to thee. We would sacrifice for thee. We
would give of our means, our time, our love, to
serve thee and our fellow men. Help us, we pray,
that this be not lip service alone, but true work-
able service, wholly acceptable unto thee. We ask
it in Jesus' name. Amen.

3

The Church Today

And I say also unto thee, That thou art Peter, and upon this rock I will build my church; and the gates of hell shall not prevail against it.
—Matt. 16:18

Behold, I lay in Zion for a foundation a stone.
—Isa. 28:16

HERE, INDEED, is strong language, but no stronger than the church's eternal foundation that runs deeper than the earth and stands firmer than granite—so firm that the powers of the invisible world are impotent to destroy it, and the invisible world, try as it will, try as it has, cannot shake it one iota.

It is interesting to note in Adam Clarke's excellent commentary the explanation of the above verses. He says that the Christ was acknowledging Peter as one of his disciples. He was speaking of the stone laid in Zion. Therefore he did not say, "On thee, Peter, will I build my church"; but changed the expression immediately and said, "Upon this rock I will build," to show that he was addressing neither Peter nor any other disciple.

Our Church today stands unshaken and sure upon that Christ-embedded rock. The church buildings erected by man may be blown to bits from high explosives from the skies, but unfailingly, up from their everlasting foundation, stone by stone, their walls will lift again, and their spires will climb unhindered toward heaven.

The worshipers today throng the doors of the church. They bow in heartfelt prayer; they sing the Lord's praises; they go quietly to receive the bread and the wine that offering hands hold out to satisfy their hunger and to quench their thirst —the nameless hunger and thirst that mankind has ever known and that only the Christ can satisfy.

The church today is serving its great purpose because the Lord wills it so. It is vitally alive— alive to the desperate need and the many problems of a perplexed and bewildered people, who are more and more turning to its doors for help and strength in these troubled times.

They will continue to come if the preacher stands in his pulpit and lifts Christ up, preaching fearlessly and glorifying Christ as he should be glorified. "And I," says Christ, "if I be lifted up from the earth, will draw all men unto me." The Word is being fulfilled today as never before.

A minister who preaches the straight gospel, who does not gloss over sin, who probes into the deep underlying meaning of the Word of God, will not find the pews of his church empty. Hearts everywhere are so willing to learn, so eager to accept Christ as their Saviour.

The church today, as it has ever been, is the answer to the soul's deep need; and never has that need been so great, so clamoring.

The leader has a responsibilty answerable to God himself. The church-school leaders must be expert miners, delving into the unsearchable riches of the Holy Word to bring forth its pure gold to others. Laymen have a definite task of bringing in those who are outside the church and introducing them to their Saviour. All of us—preacher, teacher, layman—must ever keep in mind that we are a "peculiar people." Unless we truly are "peculiar," we are no different from the great mass of the unsaved. If we are not "peculiar" in the Lord's sight, we are not of his fold but are "as sheep having no shepherd."

To be peculiar is to be different. We of the church have no business meddling with sin. We can love the sinner but must have no part in his wrongdoing. We should strive most earnestly by precept and practice to win him from his evil ways.

"What concord hath Christ with Belial? or what part hath he that believeth with an infidel? And what agreement hath the temple of God with idols? for ye are the temple of the living God; as God hath said." God's Word covers every condition of man, every circumstance surrounding him. He demands that we be a "peculiar people."

This we know—only Christ with his nail-scarred hands can ever draw the deep wounds of the world together. We find him in the church today, waiting to receive us, ready to forgive our sins and to heal our wounds.

Often there are complaints about the church by those who have failed to realize the vital place it holds in community life. Let them ask themselves what any land would be like were the churches wiped from the earth?

"Our church is costing too much," said a chronic complainer to another member of the church. "They are always asking for money. I am sick and tired of these repeated requests."

The other member replied: "I want to tell you a story out of my own life. Some years ago a little boy was born in our home, and from the time he was born he cost me money. I had to buy food and clothes, and medicine and toys,

and finally a little dog. Then he started to school,
and he cost me more. When in college he began
going with girls, and you know how much that
costs. But in his senior year in college he suddenly sickened and died, and he has not cost me
a single cent from that time on—not a single
cent."

What if our church should sicken and die?
Would we not gladly take up the burden of
expense to have it back in our midst—the place
of refuge from the storms, the spot where we
can ever be sure of meeting our Lord?

The Lord is in his holy temple. We can find
him there. Let us keep silent before him in awe
and reverence, for has he not said, "I am the
Lord that healeth thee"? Let us be healed this
day by the Lord—our souls washed clean, our
bodies freed of their many burdens, and the land
we love blest with an enduring peace.

The church should be a lighthouse in the storm:
  A beacon flung against the blackened sky,
A white, unfailing, steadfast light that shines
  For men to steer them by.

The church should be a home through these
    strange days
  Where the Bread of Life is served, and we
    can find

The Father waiting there to soothe our ills,
  And give us peace of mind.

The church should be a school where we may
      learn
  The holy truth these hours before the dawn,
That we may go equipped to meet the days
  And pass the learned truth on.

The church should be a church forevermore:
  A sure foundation and a sure reward
To all whose feet are planted on the rock
  Of Jesus Christ, our Lord.

Lord God, thou art the great physician. The
church is thy office, and we are thy patients. We
pray thee probe deeply into our wounds and bring
the complete healing we need so desperately.

May we enter thy gates with thanksgiving and
run to thy courts with praise, and entering there,
may we serve in a way that is pleasing to thee.
We ask it in Jesus' name. Amen.

4

Through God We Shall Do Valiantly

And when the servant of the man of God was risen early, and gone forth, behold, an host compassed the city both with horses and chariots. And his servant said unto him, Alas, my master! how shall we do? And he answered, Fear not: for they that be with us are more than they that be with them. And Elisha prayed, and said, Lord, I pray thee, open his eyes, that he may see. And the Lord opened the eyes of the young man; and he saw: and, behold, the mountain was full of horses and chariots of fire round about Elisha.

—II Kings 6:15-17

OUT OF the crashing thunder of these war-clouded days dare we not as a Christian nation draw courage from the above words? The Lord knows we are not Christian enough. He knows that too often in our national affairs we have had no spokesman for him, and that he has sat, an uninvited guest, at the "peace tables" of the world and has been asked for no word of guidance. He has had no part in any decision made. No prayer was offered in his name, while he alone

27

of all the earth has the power to solve the great problems of our time.

Yet as we view our great, beautiful, much-loved land and see the countless church spires climbing upward to pierce the skies, we see mute evidence of a peoples' yearning after God, their testimony of adherence to the gospel of our Lord Jesus Christ; and we can humbly feel that we are a people in many ways pleasing to him.

We have never been a marauding nation, out to rob others of their rightful heritage of territory; nor have we gone forth to lay waste and destroy for our own gain. We have ever held out a merciful hand to help the small hurt nations of the world, and this, indeed, must be pleasing to our Lord.

Therefore we should be able to lay claim to every word of encouragement offered through the Scriptures. Can we not trust that in the invisible mountains surrounding us God has set his chariots of fire and his able horsemen as a wall of protection from the enemy—that he has sent succor to bring victory out of disaster, peace out of the turmoil and strife in our day?

They that are for us are more than they that are against us. The good forces are ever at work for those who love the Lord. We are too often blinded and need to have our eyes opened to the encircling ring of fiery protection round and about us set there by the hand of God.

Often as we look about us at the evil in our midst—the crime that is rampant, the greed that is so evident, the unbridled sin running like wildfire to scorch the earth—we are inclined to cry as did the young man of old: "Alas, my master! how shall we do?"

We cry to God, our Master and our King, for guidance through this storm. We seek his wisdom to draw unto ourselves, and we pray that no encompassing host may come down upon us to destroy our land—a nation founded upon truth and righteousness by our fathers, who faltered not in their faith in Almighty God.

To all this we may well believe that our Lord speaks out: "Fear not: for they that be with us are more than they that be with them." Encouraging, hopeful words they are, spoken to cheer our hearts and to keep us strong. He would have us know that he is the great unseen force working for every nation that will honor him, keep his commandments, and trust him in time of trouble.

The great body of our nation does honor him, which gives us cause for the hope we have. We recall Abraham's earnest endeavor to save Sodom, that wicked city. "Wilt thou also destroy the righteous with the wicked?" he questioned the Lord. "Peradventure there be fifty righteous within the city: wilt thou also destroy and not spare the place for the fifty righteous that are therein? . . . Shall not the Judge of all the earth do right?" and a merciful God promised to spare the city for the fifty's sake.

Abraham, sore distressed and doubting seriously that fifty thus could be found, went on with his pleading for the wicked city. If forty were found? If thirty were found? If twenty, if ten—if there were but ten—would the Lord not save the city? He was becoming desperate in his saving efforts, and the great and good Lord who has compassion for us all—the wicked as well as the righteous—gave his promise that for the ten's sake he would not destroy Sodom.

Surely we may plead for our nation as did Abraham for Sodom. Surely in any grave crisis, any critical period in our history, we can feel free to come to the Lord with the age-old cry: "Wilt thou . . . not spare the place for the . . . righteous that are therein?" and the Lord, who is a just and righteous judge, will be as willing to do so for us as he did for his servant of old.

Why should we ever be fearful when our Lord says, "Fear not"? With him for us who can avail aught against us? Can we not with new vision lift our eyes unto the hills "from whence cometh [our] help" and see the chariots of fire ringed about us, thus enabling us to go forward as a nation to greater and better things—greater consecration to the saving Lord, greater service for other nations less fortunate? May it be so.

O righteous and Merciful God, open our blinded eyes that we may see that thou art working for all who will stay their hearts on thee. There are other calamities beside war to threaten thy people, other enemies that lay in wait to destroy.

May we be so grounded in thee that none of these things can move us or destroy our faith in thee.

We pray for all lands. Some way may the leaders' eyes be opened, and may every knee bow and every tongue be loosed to sing forth thy praises. Amen.

5

Stay Upon God

Who is among you that feareth the Lord, that obeyeth the voice of his servant, that walketh in darkness, and hath no light? let him trust in the name of the Lord, and stay upon his God.
—Isa. 50:10

THE EARNEST conning of the Bible is like studying the stars. It is like going into a meadow on an early summer evening and looking long and far into the heavens to find God's silver worlds as they appear in all their radiant splendor.

The first stars are there in their place. They are expected, and we take them more or less as a matter of course. They are like the familiar words of the Lord, known and loved by us since childhood—words that as we grew older, the heart came to over and over, and ever found them comforting. They are the evident, the importuning words, long loved from Christ's teaching.

Then suddenly, as one stands facing skyward, there are other stars that prick their way through the dusk, seemingly from nowhere—beautiful stars, hitherto unnoted. They make themselves evident only after long steadfast gazing. They are like the Word of God that holds countless glories he has hidden for all seeking ones to find.

We come upon those words possibly in some darkened hour when our need is great. After long scanning they prick their way into our consciousness and become things of light and beauty.

We come upon the above words of scripture perhaps having given them no special thought before, and there unexpectedly we find one of God's stars shining above the meadows of the world to light us on our way. It holds much in its meaning. It contains two questions, and an answer is given, which sets the whole in its clearest light.

"Who is among you that feareth the Lord, . . . that walketh in darkness, and hath no light?"

And the answer comes: "Let him trust in the name of the Lord, and stay upon his God."

Simple questions, and simple answers for the wayfarer, often bewildered, blinded, and perplexed with the conflicts in the world and in himself. The voice of Jesus would solve his problem. "Come unto me, all ye that labour and are heavy laden, and I will give you rest." These are the words to which we should hearken.

There are many walking today in darkness—the heathen who have never been told, the sinners who have not yet found the Lord, and, alas, many Christians, whose pathways should be brightened by the Son of God going on before them, shedding his light along their way. Too often they are found stumbling and faltering as they journey.

What should be done about all this? The ones who have not yet heard of the saving power of Jesus should be told. The unsaved should be saved, and the Christian should be so busy doing these things that there would be no time for brooding self-analysis, for apprehension and discouragement.

Our Lord does not want his followers to walk among the shadows. He says: "He that followeth me shall not walk in darkness." Yet he knows our feeble frames, he "remembereth that we are dust," and he understands and forgives our weakness, and looks down in tender pity upon us all.

There may be many sincere penitents, walking in darkness, wavering as they go; and they have no light, for they have not yet heard enough of the Word of God to carry it as a lantern in their hand. They are to study the Word, and they are to trust and believe in the Lord Jesus. He will be their great teacher, their unfailing guide.

We all need his staying power. It is there to be

had for the asking, but it is ours to do the
staying and we will then be kept safe although
the way apparently is dark indeed. It is a matter
of trust, a matter of faith. These can be developed
with practice.

Isaiah 50:10 is truly one of the stars in the
firmament of God's Word. It holds vital meaning for us all. Shall we not heed it, and help
others to heed it? Shall we not cry aloud to the
sinner? "Come, stay upon God, and he will forgive your sins and remove them forever from
you." Should we not plead with the fearful ones?
"Stay upon your God; he is able to banish fear
from your heart. Try him and see."

To those who are discouraged we should speak
most gently, for we, too, have known discouragement. We would bid them, too, to stay upon
God. He is a rock through any storm. Wait upon
him and the darkness will lift. To the suffering
ones let us go with infinite understanding and
say: Stay upon God. He is your refuge and your
fortress, an ever-present help in trouble. He will
sustain you.

"Who is he among you that feareth the Lord,
    That walketh in darkness, and that hath no
        light?"
A lifted voice cries out from the Holy Word

To those who are groping blindly through the
  night.
And then like a torch planted high above earth's
  sod
Comes the light of hope: "Let him stay him on
  his God."

"Let us trust in the name of the Lord." The
  words how brief,
  Yet wise are they with the wisdom of a seer;
And those who heed them will find beyond belief
  That the darkness will lift and the tangled
  paths will clear.
Let him trust in the name of the Lord for every
  need,
And "stay upon his God." Wise words, indeed!

Our Lord and our God, forgive us, thy children,
who too often walk in darkness when thou art the
light of the world, sent here to light our way. Help
us to strengthen our own faith, so that our trust in
thee will be unfaltering and unfailing. Help us to
stay upon thee, for thou art our only hope, our
only salvation. We ask it in Jesus' name. Amen.

6

The Powerhouse

The Lord thy God in the midst of thee is mighty.
—Zeph. 3:17

IT WOULD be intensely interesting to know how many earthly pilgrims throughout the ages have come upon these particularly meaningful words, have been startled by them, and have found themselves suddenly revitalized. How many have been strengthened to travel more valiantly upon their journey to eternity because of this positive assurance?

To feel the full impact of the words is to become conscious of a power, hitherto undreamed of, that is working within one's self. Too often we grow timorous. We feel we must go forward in our own strength, fearful of the "lions" in the way and ever conscious of our human frailties. All this seriously impedes our progress.

Not one of us is strong enough in himself to meet life's vicissitudes without the help of God. We cannot move confidently down the years without this inner force working for us, and yet so often we are not aware of that power. We are not supposed to attempt to go alone. We are to lay hold of that inner force loosed in our beings and in our behalf. All who do so will find an inexhaustible strength emanating from it.

Our bodies are the powerhouse in which God works. Their very intricacies prove this. Our souls are his domain. There is no possible failure on his part. His power is ours to draw upon constantly. We are to appropriate it for hourly and daily use. There are no mechanical defects in his "plant"—no sudden failure of the light that is there to guide us on our way.

We might call it the "riches of his grace"—riches that are held out to us freely and fully. Paul expresses it perfectly when he says: "Not I, but Christ." God controlling, Christ moving for us! As we take hold of that power, fear vanishes. When we falter through indecision, the right decision will be made for us. When we stumble on our journey, a steadying hand will reach out to stay us. We can move confidently, heads held high, alert to life and its glorious possibilities.

We will become conscious of the untraversed countries in our own beings. The power within us will impel us onward and upward in our discovery. We will have strength for the steepest climb, the highest pinnacle of endeavor.

There will be paths to clear that have been overrun with the brambles in the wilderness of our often fruitless wanderings—paths that when cleared will open up onto the broad highways of life which will make simpler and easier our radiant questings. We will find within ourselves a greater tolerance for others, a kindness and understanding hitherto unknown. Sympathy will leap up in our hearts like a clear wayside spring to heal and bless those who stop to drink thereof.

"The Lord thy God in the midst of thee is mighty." We take the inner look and find him there at work. With his power we can take trials and make them into victories. We can use a dark experience to make a bright one. From discouragement and seeming defeat we can learn the patience of unanswered prayer. Every disappointment can be met with hope; every doubt can be defeated by faith. Thank God this force will enable us to go on our way trustingly when one who has traveled with us, and whom we have loved more dearly than life itself, suddenly stops and takes the "shorter road home."

We have been told that the peasants in the Old Country have a saying when some particular event occurs that shadows their going: "There's never a nettle without its dock," and they go seeking for the dock in faith that they will find it. May we so lay hold of the inner force at work within us that we are driven to find healing for body and soul, and may it stir us to work diligently for the "universal good."

Let us go further into the understanding of this great truth. We read: "The Lord thy God in the midst of thee is mighty; he will save, he will rejoice over thee with joy; he will rest in his love, he will joy over thee with singing."

Think of the Almighty rejoicing over us! Think of his promise to save! Think of resting in his love! And is not the climax of this word like the culminative climb of a great oratorio? Hark! "He will joy over thee with singing." Surely here are light and glory shed upon all who have found favor in his sight. May it be you; may it be I.

We thank thee, our heavenly Father, for the boundless reaches of thy love and for thy care that is ever about us. May we be fully conscious of thy wonder-working power, and may we lay hold upon it for our good and for thy glory. We ask it in our Lord Jesus' name. Amen.

7

Brotherhood

And it shall come to pass, that whosoever shall call on the name of the Lord shall be delivered.
—Joel 2:32

The promise holds for all earth's creed and kinds,
    For every race of men beneath the sun.
Christ's "Whosoever" is a link that binds
    Us all together, and that makes us one.
Deliver, Lord, all those who call on thee.
O men, that promise holds for you and me!

THIS MATTER of brotherhood can be summed up in the one word "whosoever." In it Christ envelopes all mankind. He does not use the titles "rich and poor, high and low, black and white," for there is no discrimination in his cataloguing of humanity. He is our Father; we are his children; all men are our brothers. It is as simple as that.

The much-discussed civil rights of our day are one of his considerations. To him what is right for one is right for all. He goes to the root of the matter, and from that root there springs a great truth. He wants us to grow upward and outward "like a tree planted by the rivers of water, that bringeth forth his fruit in his season." He desires the first fruits from his people. He needs every good thing in his magnificent plan.

Had we been more conscious of that plan, had we had more of the spirit of Christ in our hearts, there would be none of the baffling problems of today. Had we been of one mind with our Lord, there would be no oppression, no discrimination against any of his people.

Men of all nations—the white, the black, the yellow—have the same emotions tugging at their hearts. There is the same hunger for betterment and understanding—and for justice. Oh, above all for justice! There is the same heartbreak in us all over failure to attain the heights for which we strive, the same despair that follows as we sink backward after our heroic and often futile efforts. Why should we not have complete understanding and sympathy one with another when we are so akin?

Let us be wise to our own faults and patient with the frailties of others. The races of today are making a supreme struggle to gain headway in the affairs of the earth. They cry aloud for freedom from oppression, freedom from bondage, freedom from prejudice. They scan the far horizon for the dawn of a new day—and it does not come.

What are we going to do about it? Are we not to work with our Lord to bring "oneness" to the peoples of the earth? Are we not through snobbery and prejudice delaying that day?

We need much to pray. We need to work. We need tolerance in our everyday living. We need to be prayed for. For our encouragement we recall on of the most stupendous things that has ever happened to us. We remember with reverence and awe that Jesus himself prayed directly for us before his crucifixion—a prayer that has lasted throughout the ages and can still be a working force in our lives.

He said, "Neither pray I for these alone, but for them also which shall believe on me through their word; that they all may be one." Wonder of wonders! Christ prayed for us. He prayed for you, and he prayed for me. In that brief prayer he prayed for the humblest Negro, the most poverty-stricken Chinese, the richest Jew, the highest honored king. He prayed for all to whom the missionaries of earth have, and will bring, the good tidings of salvation. He prayed that we all may be one.

This does not sound as if any race has the supremacy over another in God's sight, or a better opportunity than another to gain the kingdom of heaven. The basis for brotherhood is that belief—a belief in one God.

Believing on him and doing the things he commands us to do, we will heed his urgent words to "go tell my brethren." It is our task to go or to send and bring all men from every corner of the earth to a definite knowledge of the true and living God, that they may believe and that they all may be one.

There is no supreme race, although often in our arrogance and pride we may have thought ourselves to be. Given the same opportunities for advancement, the same length of time for accomplishment that we have had, any race might have equalled us or surpassed us. God has no patience with bigotry. He rejected the Pharisee who stood praying, thanking God that he was not like other men. He accepted the publican's petition and was pleased with his humility.

We are told in I John 2:10-11 that "he that loveth his brother abideth in the light, and there is none occasion of stumbling in him. But he that hateth his brother is in darkness, . . . and knoweth not whither he goeth, because that darkness hath blinded his eyes."

Is not love the solution of our problems today, and are not hatred and pride our downfall? Far too long the darkness of prejudice has blinded our eyes, and we have truly walked in darkness.

If through God's help we can be freed from our own peculiar bondage of wrong thinking, if we love enough and have charity enough, we can move unfalteringly forward unto a light hitherto unseen, knowing at last where we are going, which most certainly will be toward a city, "Eternal in the heavens." God grant it may be in the great and goodly company of our brothers and sisters from every walk of life—from the east, the west, the north, the south—who have come to believe on the Christ through the word of his followers down the years—all one at last, all true and beloved brothers, all gentle, loving sisters.

Our heavenly Father, we thank thee that thou hast prayed for us. Help us ever to bear in mind thy great encompassing love, not alone for us, but for the whole world; and may we take on that same spirit of love for our fellow men, until through the Word they may come to know thee, that we may be as one. We ask it in Christ's name. Amen.

8

Serving Our Generation

> For David, after he had served his own genera-
> tion by the will of God, fell on sleep.
> —Acts 13:36

> Blessed is the man that feareth the Lord, that
> delighteth greatly in his commandments. . . . The
> generation of the upright shall be blessed.
> —Ps. 112:1, 2

THESE BRIEF words cover the entire saga of
a great and noble personage who once sojourned
for a time upon the earth. After his passing it is
stated simply that "he had served his own
generation." Surely he served it well, or his name
would not have come down so luminously
through the centuries.

Would that the same high tribute could be
paid us all on that day when we too "fall on
sleep." Would that across the history of mankind
it could be written of us that we also served
well our time before we departed upon our far
journey to eternity.

The present should be of vital concern to us. It is all of time that we can call our own. We have nothing whatsoever to do with yesterday and nothing at all to do with tomorrow. We stand, as it were, between two eternities, the past and the future, with the latter rushing toward us and the past flowing backward like some swift bright stream with never a moment's blockage. This hour alone belongs to us, and wise, indeed, is he who clear-eyed sees and evaluates the present's vast importance.

We catch our first glimpse of David as a youth. He was daily in the fields tending his father's sheep. He was not a simple stolid country lad. He did his work well, but other vital things were occupying his heart and clamoring at his mind. There were unseen forces at work; there were intangible things for which he was ever searching. The twang of his harp strings must have echoed sweet and goldenly upon the bright thin air as he strove to capture the sound of the wind through the meadow grasses, and he was impelled to catch the swish and toss of the blowing wheat, the sound of clear water over stones. Ever within his heart there was a singing —strange songs like the beat of waves against his breast, songs of the great Jehovah, who, unknown to him at the time, was calling him across far distances to active service. Indeed, here was something urgent, something that never let him rest!

Thus unconsciously he began serving his generation, for without the artist, the poet, the musician, the world would be a strangely empty place, and many fine things would be lost.

David was preparing for his future work when the psalms he would sing would ring down the centuries to lift and inspire and strengthen hearts for higher and better living—psalms that have affected the past and will affect all future generations. In serving his own time he served all time.

But he was more than an artist with words. He was a man of war, but always for the right. He was a man of destiny. He lived close to God. He knew the agony that sin can bring. He knew the miracle of forgiveness. He was humbled to the dust, he was raised to earthly splendor, yet he acknowledged ever the majesty of God, his King. As he went about his business, his prayer was ever simple and sincere: "Let the words of my mouth, and the meditation of my heart, be acceptable in thy sight, O Lord, my strength, and my redeemer." Thus he would plead his worthy cause.

He was concerned for the Lord. He moved through his days cognizant of the everlasting goodness of his maker. He shouted aloud to his fellow men: "Declare his glory among the heathen, his wonders among all people." Was this not the missionary spirit carried like a light through the darkness? Was it not a call to true service? He cried often for men to praise the Lord. "O give thanks unto the Lord; for he is good; for his mercy endureth for ever." Was he not one of the world's first evangelists? Was he not God's man? He surely served his Lord, falling and rising again, ever singing his minor notes of repentance and his golden songs of victory until he "fell on sleep."

We each have an appointed time here on earth, and what we do with that time is a matter of eternal importance. It is a rare privilege to labor constructively, to go about doing good— lifting a burden, speaking the helpful word, living beautifully, worthily, gladly. May we serve our generation and at last, as did David, "fall on sleep," to be awakened by a voice of commendation: "Well done, thou good and faithful servant, . . . enter thou into the joy of thy Lord."

Our heavenly Father, we would be conscious of the value of time and of our relationship to it. We would serve in a way that would be pleasing unto thee. Only thus can we share in the great eternal plan, that small parts be joined together to make a perfect whole. Be our guide, we pray thee, and our instructor. We ask it in thy Son Jesus' name. Amen.

9

What of the World?

He was in the world, and the world was made by him, and the world knew him not.
—John 1:10

For God so loved the world, that he gave his only begotten Son, that whosoever believeth in him should not perish, but have everlasting life.
—John 3:16

WE LIVE in a universe so vast that striving to comprehend distance, light-years, and endless space, the mind reels under the impact. Yet it simmers down to this: our world in which we live, and which seems so boundless to our finite minds, is a very little orb, swimming in a great sea of space. In the light of the sun and moon and stars it is but a speck among the constellations, yet—marvel of marvels!—God so loved the world that he sent his only Son with a torch of light and a book of truth to save it from destruction.

In creating the earth he separated the land by

far reaches of sea. No doubt he did it thus for
the great cause of peace. He knew his people
and how difficult it is for men to live together in
unison. He made the different races and impar-
tially meted to each a natural habitat. He is a lover
of peace; at his advent that was made clear. He
wisely separated the hemispheres. To the continents he gave a dividing isthmus.

He wanted peace. How his great heart must
ache today over the world with its tumult and
strife, its wars and rumors of wars, its greed and
its hatreds!

We must bear in mind that he loves all races,
that we are not his special favorites. Remember-
ing this we will be more tolerant of others. The
yellow men, the black men, the white men are
all his children. The nationalities have no dividing line in the heart of the Father. His children
are quarreling today. They have fought throughout the centuries for more power, more territory,
more recognition. Men have constantly been at
one another's throats. There have been aggressors
and defenders, the hunter and the hunted, the
victor and the conquered; and all the while, instead, we should have been seeking "first the
kingdom of God." Those who do so have God's
unbreakable promise that all things that are for
our good shall be "added unto" us.

We have bartered for such paltry things

throughout the ages. Why do we do it? Earth shall pass away, Christ says, but my word shall not pass. How ephemeral are the things for which men have fought and died. Oh, that we would ever be laying hold of enduring things!

War—how horrible, how wasteful, how useless! It brings only untold suffering and agonizing sorrow, and the laying waste of the good earth that is our heritage. War—that spells only disaster and ruin!

What shall we do about it today? The Bible tells us that "at the name of Jesus every knee should bow, of things in heaven, and things in earth, and things under the earth." We note the words "should bow." Why should we come at some future time? Now is the time. Now is the day of salvation. Let us hasten to come to the only source of help left to us as nations and as individuals. Oh, may we be quick about it— quick to seek forgiveness, for our sins have been many. He has promised to forgive and not upbraid us. Let us make haste in this matter of forgiveness. May we forgive as we hope to be forgiven.

Shall we not pray for God's kingdom to be established upon the earth and then help in every way we can to bring it to pass? Only through repentance and through a return to the teachings of Jesus Christ can we be saved spiritually and physically in these awful threatening days. The hounds are upon us. Their cries rend the air! There is only one way of return, and that is the way that leads directly to the feet of Jesus. Why do we wait? One wonders.

What of the world if the nations crumble?
  What of the helpless and forlorn
Left to their fate to starve and stumble
  Over the earth that greed has torn
Wide with its fangs of hate and fury?
  Where is the tongue with the power to tell
What the destruction, and where the jury
  Wise to ponder these acts of hell?

How will God speak through the crashing
    thunder?
  How will he judge mankind at last
After the ruin of earth's bright wonder,
  After his proffered chance is past?
What of the world if the nations fail him,
  And men walk on in their own proud might?
O my brothers, bow down and hail him,
  And pray that his mercy may stay this night!

Our great Creator and our God, we are of the world. We are in part responsible for much of the evil that has come upon us. We come to thee. We fall at thy feet, praying for forgiveness. Without thy help the whole world is lost.

O Lord God, some way save us. Bring peace out of turmoil. Give beauty for ashes and the oil of joy for mourning. Let peace follow the awful ache and pain in our hearts this day. We do not deserve these things we ask for, but may thy grace be sufficient to bring them to pass. We ask it in Jesus' name. Amen.

10

Bravery

Be strong and of a good courage, fear not, nor be afraid . . . : for the Lord thy God, he it is that doth go with thee; he will not fail thee, nor forsake thee.—Deut. 31:6

BACK OF all true bravery there is some kind of faith—faith that right will win, faith in one's self to carry through any difficulty; but more often it is a steadfast faith in God and his promises that gives high courage to the human heart.

Bravery is a splendid virtue wherever it is found. There is ever something of the Christ encompassed in it. We see it in many places these days. It is in the eyes of young boys as they move out to meet the unknown in war-rocked lands. We see it in the faces of mothers, who acknowledge when asked, "Yes, I have a son in service," or, "My son is of draft age; he will soon be going." We see bravery in men's bearing as they square their shoulders for greater and heavier burdens they must bear.

We watch all these lay hold of the bright shield of faith with which to gird themselves for the days ahead. Yet there are those who are braver still. These are the ones who take on the courage of Christ that day in the garden, his endurance at Calvary; for they too in a way are being crucified. They are the patient Christian sufferers in the world who daily fight the enemy pain. Theirs is a harder fight than those have who face the wild excitement of battle. Theirs is an unapplauded fight. They do not march to music. They battle with a foe that gives no quarter, day or night. There are times when the keen bayonets of pain all but wound mortally, those days when the lurking foe tortures by striking on two fronts—the body and the mind, which grows naturally oppressed with suffering.

But through this very suffering they have learned to understand others who are fighting their own great battles. They are keened with sympathy. Let no one imagine they are indifferent to the agony of the entire world in these days. It breaks their hearts, and they often feel helpless to serve in any way; but they do serve— much better than they know. They have the time to pray. They have understanding hearts, and God, who is proud of them, listens and hears their prayers.

It is difficult for them to remember that "they

also serve who only stand and wait," or that those who are bidden to "stay by the stuff" are doing as great a work as those who go forth to battle. They have stayed so closely at the Lord's side that they know him most intimately and therefore can pray better than many others. Their prayers reach the heart of God, and they will be answered.

These are the silent warriors. Their lips smile for the sake of others; their tongues guard their secrets well. Often they give out the shining stuff of courage, gathered on their own stark battlefield, to those bewildered ones in their first baffling experience with suffering and sorrow.

Preachers and laymen alike come to them for wisdom and understanding, and they never go away unblest and uncomforted. The Lord must look down on all battlefields with infinite sadness and sorrow, but I am sure he straightens proudly before such heroism as this. He recognizes these as his kin; these are the ones to whom he has trusted much. He knows not everyone is worthy of such a trust.

There is a purpose in suffering. God does not send it to any of us, but he permits it to work a good work in a patient, unrebellious sufferer. We recall that Jesus said in his own great agony: "Thinkest thou that I cannot now pray to my Father, and he shall presently give me more than twelve legions of angels? But how then shall the scriptures be fulfilled, that thus it must be?" God has his helpers on the earth. There would be no such thing as sympathy in any heart if there were no suffering. He tells us to comfort one another, and how could we do so unless we had gone the same dark road that others are treading?

These suffering ones realize that they should not be favored above their Lord; surely they, too, are given the grace to wait the fulfillment of his purpose in their lives. Otherwise they could not go on.

The Lord can remove all suffering with the touch of his gentle healing fingers, but he does not always do so. He knows that we are better soldiers for the testings and that through suffering we can become like him. He suffered, he endured, and he knows well the cost of that endurance. He notes courage wherever it may be found, and we may be sure that he writes each patient burden-bearer's name down in the book of life in illuminated letters, and after each name he writes the one word, "victor."

The following incident is a true example of real bravery and courage. A young soldier on week-end leave stood on a bleak street corner in London, homesick and despairing, when suddenly from a basement window there lifted on the air a burst of bird song, so clear and piercingly sweet that the lad was immediately transported by its wizardry back to his southern home in America. He was hearing again a mockingbird singing from the highest tip of the magnolia tree in the garden.

Surely no mockingbird could be caged in that dingy English basement, yet there it came again: the high trill, the triumphant gladness of the bird he knew and loved so well. The impulse to follow the song was too strong, and the lad descended the steps and found there, not a sleek-plumaged songster, but a human bird. A tailor, seated at his workbench, arose courteously and came limping forward. "What can I do for you, sir?" he asked.

"You can tell me where you learned to whistle so beautifully and what is the inspiration."

A faint smile brushed the man's lips. "From an aching leg," he said. "You see, I picked up a bit of shrapnel in the last war, and my leg seldom gives me much ease."

"But the music was filled with light—and gladness," the boy stammered.

"Why not? Gladness and light are all about us if we have the eyes to see them, and pain should not blind us to them. I have often thought that a sufferer knows more of the essence of joy than do the free ones. At any rate one may as well whistle as to complain. It really takes less energy."

"And yet you are able to send out hope and inspiration to the men above in the street!" the young man marveled.

"Pain usually does something to one. It makes a person break silence," the man said as his smile broadened. "Whistling has become a sort of habit with me, and I whistle when my leg forgets to ache as well as when it is at its worst. Surely folks like to listen to it better than if I groaned all the while."

"Indeed they do, sir! You have heartened me more than I can say. I came down here feeling mighty discouraged, and I am going away much better. Thank you for helping me." The boy turned and made his way into the dampness and fog of the London street, bearing within his heart the echo of the light-hearted songbird of his homeland.

Our heavenly Father, we are thy children and are often prone to discouragement and fear. Help us to face every issue of life bravely, knowing that thou hast promised to be with us through our adversities. May we be so courageous through trials and afflictions that thou wilt be proud of us rather than ashamed. We need thy hourly, daily help as we journey; then truly we can be brave of heart and ready for any contingency. Amen.

11

The Lord Knows

But he knoweth the way that I take: when he hath tried me, I shall come forth as gold.
—Job 23:10

Lord, thou knowest all things.—John 21:17

THERE ARE few of us who have not at one time or another been "tried," and often seemingly beyond our endurance. We moan, we cry, we fret under some strange hurting experience; we strive desperately to get out from under the chafing burden weighing so heavily upon us.

We fail to wait for the hand of the Lord to ease that burden and for the road to grow smooth before our troubled eyes. We do not take the long view and realize that often God tests us to try our mettle and to strengthen our faith. Mettle is tested by fire, even as is the metal from the earth's mines; and faith grows stronger if we have the will and the courage to wait for the evidence of the Lord's steadying hand.

After the testing we can truly "come forth as gold," bright and shining from the crucible. Then only can we see his purpose clearly, and we can praise him for the trials through which we have passed. We may be sure, and thus strengthened, that whatever befalls us, the Lord knows the why of it all; and as Peter of old on that spring morning on the shore of Galilee replied to the Lord's persistent questioning, we too can cry aloud, "Lord, thou knowest all things."

One noon a young man was walking slowly down a city street, his entire attitude one of defeat. Hands in pockets, feet dragging, despondency written clearly on his face, he turned a corner and came suddenly upon an old friend, a retired businessman, on his way to lunch.

"Hello, Timothy," the man accosted him. "How are you? But say, what's the matter? You look as if the skies had fallen."

"They have," the youth replied. "They surely have."

"Come in here with me, and let's have lunch together. We can talk things over in a quiet corner."

"Now tell me," the friend said as they settled to their lunch.

"Well," Timothy exclaimed, "the Lord knows what I am going to do now! I'm through. The place where I have been working was too big for me, or I was too little for it—whichever way you care to put it. I was afraid of it from the first. The work wasn't what I had expected it to be, and I just couldn't make it. The manager found out about it, and, well, I'm finished, that's all. I really worked hard at the job, and I did my best, but my best wasn't good enough." His voice trailed off.

The elder man looked at him thoughtfully, giving him his undivided attention. Then he said, "I like the way you began this talk, Timothy. I noticed you said, 'The Lord knows.'"

The young man flushed. "That was just a figure of speech, I suppose. I ought not to have said it—I really did not mean it. I meant that I am down and out, and I have no idea what I am going to do now, and nobody knows how tough it is."

"Yes, somebody knows, Timothy; and why should you not say it and mean it? The Lord knows, for he does know. It is an unalterable fact that the Lord knows our every step. He does know what you are going to do. He sees the entire journey you are taking from birth to death. He sees the end, and you only see the way. Too often we go stumbling along in our own puny strength and with our faulty judgment, while all the time he is willing and ready to hold out a directing hand. We are both professing Christians, Timothy. We belong to the same church. We belong to One who knows our every need, our every desire, and our every purpose. Why should we not cling to the fact that we have a Lord who knows and who understands."

He continued, "I know I am talking at length, but I want to say that his power is working in you and with you toward your destiny, which no doubt will be bright if you do your part. Perhaps the work you have been doing would not be for your ultimate good. Unquestionably he has something better awaiting you, and some day you will thank him for putting this seeming barrier in your way. Say it often, Timothy: 'The Lord knows.' It will be a comfort to you and strength for you as you go your way with God's help to find the right place for your particular talents. Those talents, I know, and better still God knows, are unusual. No matter what has happened today, this seeming calamity has not been purposeless. Bear that in mind."

"Go home, Timothy," his friend continued. "You are tired. You probably have tried too hard to be a square peg in a round hole. Rest awhile.

Pray for guidance, and you will get it. This is certain."

The lad sat still a moment, and then slowly —in a half whisper—he repeated the words, savoring their vital meaning: "The Lord knows what I am going to do." The petulance was gone from his voice, his face took on a new light, and his shoulders squared visibly. "That's a mighty big thing to think about, isn't it?" he said. "If he knows, he understands; and in that case he would not keep a thing from me that I need so much—the right work, the advancement I so want. I just must have started out on the wrong foot."

"You are right, Timothy; God knows. He cares. He knows what you are going to do, and he will help you with it. That should be encouragement enough for one day."

So whether we are young or old, whether we are in the valley or on the mountaintop, shall we not keep in mind the undeniable truth that God knows, he loves, he cares? Even though we are lost at times and bewildered in a maze of seemingly insurmountable difficulties, there is certainty somewhere; and it is not God's way to leave his children lost and distressed if they but come to him for help and guidance. His hand is there; reach for it. And say it often: "The Lord Knows."

Our Lord and our God, we are grateful beyond words for the assurance of thy loving care. Thou knowest the way that we take, and, dear Lord, may we, when we are tried, come forth as gold in thy sight.

Help us, when we grow discouraged, to turn to thee in trusting faith. Free us from useless worry, and make us conscious of thy love, knowing that it is ever working for us and for our good. We ask it in Jesus' name. Amen.

12

The Root of Courage

He shall not fail nor be discouraged.
—Isa. 42:4

THE ROOT of courage is faith—faith in Almighty God and faith in ourselves as the children of God.

Discouragement, we know, is the antithesis of courage. It is a far backtracking in our spiritual living. Satan, we may be sure, delights in seeing us bowed down under that self-inflicted burden. He knows that its weight impedes our progress. It robs the heart of joy, and it makes us ready victims for his blandishments. But to his chagrin there is One he cannot touch—One who has faith in the right, who proclaims that "all things work together for good" to those who love him, and nothing can shake that faith.

No sane-minded person today would call out as did Pippa, the little Italian maid:

> God's in his heaven:
> All's right with the world.

God is in his heaven—never doubt it—but, alas! the world through sin and greed and corruption is in great and frightening peril. Even so, the Creator will not let it dispirit him. He holds the reins in his hands; nothing is beyond his control, and his will eventually will be done. It is ours to pray, to work, to teach, to "go" as he bade us go, and then to wait for the fulfillment of his Word.

Wise are we if we can look out and beyond the confusion of our day to see that we are workers together for good, and to have faith that even out of this darkness our Father will bring light. Oh, let us cling to the fact that he has faith in us. We cannot fail him. He does not grow discouraged, and we should not.

Some years ago there was a young lad having a very difficult time with his arithmetic lessons. He was distressed and mortified over his seeming failure. One afternoon when school was dismissed, he stayed on, trying to work out a particularly difficult problem. The teacher, in striving to bring order to the deserted room, did not at once notice him sitting there in a far corner. Finally she saw him and wondered about it. She asked him to come up to her desk.

"What's the matter, Jimmie? What is it?" she asked.

With tears in his eyes and a lump in his throat the boy replied, "I can't do it—it's just no use! I don't understand a thing I am trying to do. I don't want the other boys to laugh at me for being so dumb—they seem to know what's it's all about."

"Let me see your paper," said the teacher. "See, this part is right."

"Maybe it is, but I don't know how it got that way, and the rest is all wrong."

"No, here is another place that is almost right. You began well. You made only a slight mistake, so let us correct it and go on from there."

To be sure, in that brief while the teacher had not shown the boy how to work all the problems. He was too tired and discouraged to see clearly what she was trying to teach him, but this much he knew and understood—she was trying to help him, and she had confidence in his ability to master those baffling problems.

"She believes I can do it! She believes I can do it, and I almost believe I can, now. I see a little what she means. She's swell, and she has faith in me!" His lifting heart took up the words like a refrain. That the teacher was not discouraged with him rebuked his own discouragement and gave him power to succeed. He was not an exceptionally brilliant scholar, but he was a faithful student, and the encouragement given him was the impetus he needed to go on with renewed zeal.

Years afterward in a time of great perplexity and doubt that afternoon came back to him. He had suffered reversals, and his faith had been sorely tried. He was tempted to give up. Then one day he came across these prophetic words: "He shall not fail nor be discouraged."

"I wonder if God has faith in me." he thought. "It seems to mean that very thing. It says here: 'A bruised reed shall he not break, and the smoking flax shall he not quench. . . . He shall not fail nor be discouraged.' "

His own spiritual lamp had been burning dimly; it had given out smoke instead of illumination. He had been bruised through misunderstanding and wronged by those he thought were his friends.

"Can God tape up a bruised reed? Can he fill a lamp that has burned so nearly dry?" he asked. "Would God count himself a failure if I, James Munn, should fail?" Question after question revolved in his mind. Then those words echoed back to him with the certainty of assurance: "He shall not fail nor be discouraged." It was a blessed and soul-strengthening thought.

He remembered the day he had gone to his teacher, ashamed of his tears, humiliated and defeated; and her faith had given him faith in himself. Now grown to manhood he humbly came to the great all-wise Teacher who withholds no good thing from his children, and upbraideth not, and cried: "Lord God, if you are not discouraged with me, I shall not despair of myself."

Throughout the years that followed there were many periods of despondency and depression for this man, but he would recall the vital words and they helped him, until finally the habit of courage was established and had become second nature to him. Clear hope and faith came to mark his everyday life.

What a Lord we have! How vividly he reveals himself through his Word! How willingly he reaches down and out to help us up! May we lay hold of his hand and rise to heights that as yet we know not of! He is not discouraged. We should not be.

Lord God, we are grateful that thou art our Father, our Saviour, and our example. We are humbly glad that thou dost understand our human frailties and art forgiving toward them. Help us to emulate thee in all our ways. Help us to move through failure to success, through discouragement to high courage, and thus grow through thy grace to be more like thee. Amen.

13

Like as a Father

Like as a father pitieth his children, so the Lord pitieth them that fear him.—Ps. 103:13

HERE WE have one of the most emphatic statements in God's Word. As a tender, compassionate earthly father loves his child, so even more our heavenly Father loves all who fear him, who stand in reverent awe of him, and yet who find him ever approachable, tender, and compassionate.

His love is not pictured anywhere else in a stronger, clearer light—a love more intense and pitiful than earth has ever known. He feels for us through physical suffering. Christ took on that same suffering in order to understand better that which we at times must endure. He mourns for us in our grief. Jesus wept. He knew sorrow intimately. He weeps over our sins. He lived among sinners, yet he sinned not. He goes out after the wandering lost one, for each of his children is vitally important in his sight. He forgives always. He is a noble example for any earthly father to follow in his attitude toward a wayward son.

He is far more watchful over us than the most devoted parent could possibly be. God, the Father, sent his only Son to die for us. This was a greater sacrifice than for him to have come himself, for a father would rather suffer than have his son suffer. We can trust such love. We can lean hard upon it.

Throughout the ages the fathers and the mothers have clung to this assurance of God's great abiding love for their children. When their own love seemingly has failed, their own admonitions have been disregarded, they turn to the One all-loving, all-understanding, and find comfort in his words. They come for wisdom and strength, and it is given them.

It is ours as children of a heavenly Father, and an earthly father, to love much in return. We are to be obedient. We are to heed the admonitions of the great "all-over" Father. We are to be appreciative of our parents here on earth and unsparing in our praise when it is deserved and in the voicing of our love where it is needed.

Our Lord's love becomes more evident the more we draw upon it. We need it at all times, in sickness and in health, in adversity and through days of prosperity. It is given without the asking. Truly it is a love born in heaven.

There is the story told of a beautiful young girl whose life was nearing its close. Her busy father, active in legal and political life, made hurried visits to his office, then came home day after day to be with her in her last hours.

He granted her every wish whenever possible, and it was comforting to him that she found in her religion a source of strength and comfort that robbed approaching death of any dread.

He was an upright man, but one from whom, because of his busy life, religion had been crowded out. One day as he was sitting beside his daughter's bed, she asked him to read to her. He picked up a current magazine and began reading a bit of light fiction, thinking to please her. But she soon wearied of it.

"Father," she asked, "won't you please bring my Bible and read from it?"

"Certainly, my dear," he replied, and he was glad that she had asked for it. He was a strong man with a good, well-controlled voice, and he began calmly and slowly reading the Sermon on the Mount. He knew where to find it. He knew it was good, and he read on with a growing appreciation of the sonorous beauty of the words.

The girl grew more and more restless. "Don't you like it, darling?" he asked.

"Oh, father!" she exclaimed. "It isn't what I want—about our righteousness exceeding that of the Pharisees! Please find the place and read where it says: "Like as a father pitieth his children."

The father's voice trembled a bit, but he said, "I will find it." He looked through a concordance, found the verse, and began: "Like as a father"—and he could read no further.

"Oh, my child!" he cried, "if God loves you as I do, if he feels as intensely as I"—and he put his face in his hands and wept.

The girl reached out to him. "It is the verse we both need," she said softly.

"Yes, my dear, that is what we need."

Truly it is what we all need! To whom would we turn without it? Where could comfort be found in any sorrow, any agony, without that love reaching out to envelope us?

"Like as a father. . . ."

Father, in our great need we ever turn to thee. Help us to be more worthy of thy love for us. Help us to obey thy loving commandments that are given for our good. Help us to be better children to our earthly parents, speaking the loving word, voicing our sincere appreciation, before it is too late. We ask thee for this help in Jesus' name. Amen.

14

The Stayed Mind

Thou wilt keep him in perfect peace, whose mind is stayed on thee: because he trusteth in thee.—Isa. 26:3

Great peace have they which love thy law: and nothing shall offend them.—Ps. 119:165

THE WORD "peace" means harmony, tranquillity, to be quiet, to be still; and whether between nations or in the individual heart, this is a high peak of attainment.

We are told we can have that peace by the simple act of trusting God. If we trust him implicitly, we will have peace in our souls because the Word of God says it will be so—not a passing peace but an ever-abiding peace that floods the inner being.

If we were to go about asking different persons for their definition of peace, we would no doubt receive many and varied answers. Let us try it.

We stop by the bedside of a wounded soldier. "Sir," we ask, "what is peace?" At the moment we believe he would answer: "Freedom from pain—and sleep."

We search out a Chinese sitting languidly in the sun. "Our friend, what to you is peace?" we ask, and he looks up at us from vacant eyes and answers: "The bowl of rice for this hunger."

We stop to greet an Indian walking along a dusty desert path. "Our brother, could you tell us what peace really is?" He looks away to the far horizon and with the strange wisdom of his race answers: "Peace is freedom—freedom to be myself, freedom to walk on these plains and to find, when I return, the glowing oven and the baking loaf."

The laborer coming up out of the mine at sundown, black with grime and stooped from long bending, would answer simply: "A bed at night—that is peace."

All these are good and true answers as far as they go. They come out of the depths of human and bodily needs, but what of the hunger cry of the spirit? Let us try once more.

We come upon a lowly saint of earth whose face, as he turns to us from his work, shines like the sun in the darkness. "Brother," we ask, "what to you is peace?"

Here is one who knows his God intimately.

He is in constant contact with him, and we get an answer that refreshes the soul. "Peace? Love is the answer," he replies: "love of God, love for our fellow men, love for all God's creatures. If we love enough, we can hurt no living thing. Greed and hatred cannot abide in a heart filled with love. Love can solve the problems of the earth. God is love, and love brings peace to any heart," and he turns again happily to his task.

Men seek for peace as one who is thirsty seeks for water. We crave it as the hungry crave bread. We plead for it as the street beggar pleads for money, and all the while it is there waiting for us to appropriate it, ready to be freely given from the out-pouring hand of God.

We are to trust him. We are to love him and our fellow men, and in return he trusts us and loves us, and he gives us peace, which is better than bread to the hungry or water to the thirsty. It is a quencher of thirst, food for the starving. It is rest to the soul.

Nothing can move or offend those who have this great peace in their hearts. Catastrophies may come, calamities may follow, misfortune may seemingly track them down, but peace remains, for their minds are stayed on the One all-powerful. They have tried him and have not found him wanting. They have that certain stillness said ever to be in the direct center of the whirling cyclone. The storm may roar about them, but they are at peace. They depend upon their God, and they are not afraid.

Alas, among the nations today there is no harmony, no tranquillity. God has often been ignored even in our supposedly Christian land. In some nations he is entirely nonexistent as far as their leaders are concerned. How can a people stay their minds? How can they trust One who is not there? How can our land expect his blessing of peace if we ignore the one great force that is able to bring peace out of confusion and disaster?

Strange, indeed, how the old earth blunders on, lost in the night and straining toward the dawn, hoping to find a peace that can so easily be found.

Christ came to earth to the song of peace. On earth peace, good will toward men." Summed up in that heralding is the solution of our troubles. He bids us only trust him, and out of that trust will come a peace that passeth all understanding to abide in our hearts both now and forevermore.

Can we not trust a God who loved us enough to send his Son to die for us? Is not that great sacrifice on his part proof enough of his constancy of purpose toward us? Has anyone ever found one reason to think him untrustworthy? If we stay our minds upon him, if we trust him fully, we shall have peace in our souls. If we as a nation turn in unison to God, he will turn to us and save our land. If we do not, assuredly there will be no peace.

Strange that we are so stupid and so blind not to have received fully the gift of peace that the Christ came to bring us. The star above his manger has not dimmed. The angels' proclamation of peace has not died fruitlessly upon the air. The gift may still be ours if we but lay hold upon it. Let us do so and thus know from a beautiful experience the true meaning of peace.

Our dear Lord, we would so stay our minds on thee that nothing can move us. We would trust thee fully, laying hold of thy wisdom and thy strength, that we may be fortified to meet every contingency of life. Give us quiet hearts and tranquil minds. Help us to love enough in a world that so desperately needs love. Then, we know, thy perfect peace will be ours. Help us, we pray, to please thee in all our ways. Amen.

This Wilderness

_____

The voice of him that crieth in the wilderness, prepare ye the way of the Lord, make straight in the desert a highway for our God.—Isa. 40:3

WE ARE TOLD that in the early days the eastern monarchs, when attempting a journey through the wilderness, sent out harbingers before them to prepare the way and to remove obstacles. They were to cry out encouragement when the way was cleared and to shout warning when it was not.

John the Baptist was a crier for the Lord. He went before, announcing the Lord's coming to all who would listen. He was a man born in the desert. He preached in the desert. He was strong and singularly rugged, having taken on something of his environment. He came at a time when the Jewish church was as fruitless as the land about it. He was "the voice of one crying in the wilderness, Prepare ye the way of the Lord, make his paths straight." (And how mankind failed to do so!) John with his raiment of camel's hair, his leathern girdle, his diet of locust and wild honey—John, the blood kin of our Lord—was the one fitted to "go before" the Christ, to make his way straight.

A wilderness is ever a wild and fearful place in which men are prone to lose their way. Oh, mightily we need a crier in this wilderness of today! Somehow through blind wandering we have lost the way through this trackless waste. Oh, much we need the crooked places in our national life made clear and straight and plain once more, the brambles obstructing our pathway torn away to facilitate our going, with a great Christian leader striding on before us to cry back encouragement when he can and to warn where there is need.

It is told that Abraham Lincoln's earnest childhood prayer ran thus: "God bless us all. Help my dog to keep on being a good dog, and don't let any of us get lost in the wilderness." The young country lad's heart was early made fearful of the entanglement of the wilderness that lay all about him. Always he was a crier in the wilderness. He was ever endeavoring to help men steer clear of the bogs and undergrowth that would trip them and discourage them in their forward progress.

He, like all righteous men, wanted to keep life in the clear—the distant horizons, toward which he was forging, plain before his eyes and the way marked distinctly for his feet. This he wanted for all men, and he worked toward that end. Oh, to look upon his like again!

Grateful, indeed, we should be for the one Crier who went early before us and whose voice sounds back to us across the years. He says: "This is the way, walk ye in it." "I am the way, the truth, and the life." Had men ever heeded his voice, the wilderness of earth would have long since been cleared, and we could have gone joyfully on our way. Let us cry out in answer to that voice: "Lord, we will strive to find thy footprints through this entanglement and with thy help come out into the clearing."

A man-made desert is as truly bewildering as are the great trackless wastes of nature. Men flounder in their going; they wander off, lost in a maze of a wild growth of evil, of a mirage of beckoning sands. Their search for the clear springs of the waters of truth and righteousness is an insistent, clamoring thirst in their souls. We are in such a desert today. Wars and rumors of wars have wrought a devastation all about us. The evils that follow any world-shaking event are vast and frightening. Often men at the head of a government become drunk with power and fail in their grave responsibilities. They have failed to cry aloud to their followers.

When shall "the wilderness and the solitary place . . . be glad"? When shall "the desert . . . rejoice, and blossom as the rose"? Our hearts long to know. Surely there will rise up a faithful crier who will be able to warn us of the evil ahead, to cry encouragement to us when the thorns and brambles that so detain us are cleared away. God send such a crier, then help us to help ourselves in this dark shadowed land that lies about us.

We realize that the world God made so beautifully, so perfectly, loaned to his children as a peaceful homeland, has been laid waste and despoiled by the very ones to whom he gave this marvelous legacy. Men in their greed have endeavored to push God aside. He will not be pushed. In fact the satanic threat in the world today is Communism, and Communism is a war against God—that, and that alone, is what the word means. God will be the victor—let no man think otherwise.

We have, we know, been profligate with our inherited wealth. Through selfishness we have forgotten the future generations that will need a world clear of strife and wild entanglements. We recall what Ruskin once said: "The Lord has lent us the earth for a season. It belongs as much to those who come after us as to us."

What a pity it is if we do not straighten the paths for their oncoming! What a shame if we leave them nothing but a great devastation!

Our Father, we thank thee that thou hast gone before us and that we can still hear thy voice beckoning us on. When we stumble and fall, may we rise again and go on in thy strength. Help us to clear the paths through this strange wilderness of today, that the coming generations may find the going easier, the goal ahead simpler to keep in sight. We ask it in Jesus' name. Amen.

16

Let Us Give Thanks

Sing forth the honour of his name: make his praise glorious.—Ps. 66:2

What shall I render unto the Lord for all his benefits toward me? I will take the cup of salvation, and call upon the name of the Lord. I will pay my vows unto the Lord now in the presence of all his people.—Ps. 116:12-14

"SING FORTH the honour of his name: make his praise glorious." We repeat these words as an anthem repeats its beautiful scores. They are victorious, shouting words—ones to heed.

We cannot praise without being thankful. We cannot be thankful without offering up our praise to the One to whom we are grateful. We extol our God, acknowledging his goodness, and our hearts overflow with gratitude.

What shall we render unto the Lord for all his benefits? We can take the out-held cup of salvation, we can acknowledge him as God.

We can call upon his name. We can do all this in the privacy of our own hearts, but we must go further—we must pay our vows unto the Lord "in the presence of all his people." And we must not be chary in our praise. We are sure the Lord loves sincere and honest and rapturous praise from his children.

We look in wonderment at the world about us. We see it in all its beauty and splendor. We would be aware of God's gifts of every day. We should never fail to appreciate his world and of our own accord "sing forth the honour of his name: make his praise glorious."

Let us sing a song of the earth:

Be glad for it, the goodness of the earth!
  Rejoice in it, the splendid gift of God.
So much of beauty and so much of worth
  Springs ever upward from the yielding sod.
All our possessions, table, bed, and chair,
  Are uproots from the earth's full flowing breast;
Our roof, our daily bread, the clothes we wear,
  Spring from deep roots that mankind may be
    blest.

O Hearts, let us rejoice and sing our praise
  For those good things which God has kept in
    store
Deep in the earth for need throughout our days.

God grant, although we use them more and
     more,
They may be unexhausted to bestow
     Upon the generations yet to be:
The earth's continued goodness and the flow
     Of life itself, which God's hands have set free.

How fitting it is that a nation should set apart
one day, one glorious day, for special worship
and praise. This does not mean that one day out
of a full and blessed year is sufficient time to
devote to gratitude and thanksgiving, but it is
due our God that a nation should pause as one
to thank him and "make his praise glorious."

We recall the early settlers in our land. They
had come a long and terrifying journey over untraversed seas that they might find freedom to
worship God as they knew he should be wor-
shiped. They put God first in their lives. They
were upright and honest and pleasing to him.
Can we not picture them in the autumn of the
year?—a people grateful beyond words for their
blessings yet striving to find words in prayer
with which to express their deep emotions.

The maize was gathered in. At night the stock-
ade gates were shut, and there was comparative
safety. The frost came early those New England
nights. The corn stalks rattled in the gusty wind.

The hills were on fire with scarlet and crimson foliage, where the blood in their veins had been suddenly stopped.

Partridge drummed in the distance, and a fox barked on a hill. The harvest moon rode high over the wilderness, and a resonant voice was raised in sincere thanksgiving: "For all of our blessings we offer our thanks and our praise," and the day of days was established. The voice echoed across the land and became the voice of a continent. A settlement grew and became this, our beloved nation. And still the habit clings. After the harvest in our land a people pause to express their gratitude to the God of our fathers—fathers whose faith lives yet in their children. God grant we grow into a stronger faith than we yet have known. God grant we may emulate our forefathers in the simplicity of their living, their earnestness of endeavor, their strict observance of the Sabbath, and their absolute trust.

May our thanksgiving be as sincere as theirs. We too have our own wilderness to clear, our own dangers to battle. We also have a God who is able to keep whatever we commit to his keeping. Shall we not strive to be sturdier pioneers in our own way of life? Our own harvest, for which we give thanks, goes further than the good grain that we gather in. Ours is a harvest of industry, of research and experiment. Men there are who are giving their lives for the betterment of their kind. Others are burning their candles at both ends in order that more light may be shed upon the treatment of disease, the simplifying of hard labor, the smoothing of the way for gracious and better living.

There is no end to the divine curiosity that drives us forward to the service for mankind. May our Lord bless these endeavors that are for his glory.

Our Lord and our God, we thank thee for all good things. We thank thee for the things that may not at the time seem right to us, but if we are drawn closer to thee because of them, if our wills are strengthened to move forward with thee, we truly can be grateful even for these.

We would sing forth thy praise. We would make thy praise glorious. Accept our gratitude, dear Lord, and make us worthy of thy loving care that is constantly about us. Amen.

17

The Family

God setteth the solitary in families.—Ps. 68:6

Yet setteth he the poor on high from affliction, and maketh him families like a flock.—Ps. 107:41

What makes a nation great? Not lands or gold,
  Or giant enterprise, but this fine thing
That is as old as the earth itself is old:
  The family with its gracious flowering
When children come to bless a home and make
  A haven and a heaven on the earth,
Where loyalty reigns forever for love's sake,
  And faith and trust are comrades by the
    hearth.

God, bless the families of the world who turn
  To thee for guidance. Meet their every need;
Make staunch their roofs, supply them fuel to
    burn,
  Give them thy daily bread on which to feed,
And in return, Lord, grant they may abide
As a nation's strength, its glory and its pride.

GOD APPROVES of families. He has put his special blessing upon them. Would that each related group would honor him as he honors them. Oh, that fathers and mothers would realize the vast importance of the early years of childhood, and that they would strive with God's help to mold their children into the likeness of the Christ! Would that they might ever be conscious of the blessed everydayness of living and hold the hours as a sacred trust in which to accomplish great good for eternity.

We recall the plaint of Job: "Oh that I were as in months past, . . . when my children were about me." The years go by swift as the wind, and soon, too soon, the children are grown and gone, and parents realize too late that of all the years the ones when their children were little and close about them were the best, the happiest.

If they miss the sacred privilege, the great opportunity, of rearing their children "in the nurture and admonition of the Lord," they have lost something that never can be regained. These are the productive years when the sowing must be done for the harvest of souls. If that sowing is neglected, there will be no harvest. Surely then, as of old, the wail can rend the air: "His children are far from safety."

No parent can give a child a greater legacy than Christianity—a faith in the Lord Jesus and an unshakable assurance of his companionship through life. A heritage of wealth can vanish. High social position can be lost in a day, but Christ and his friendship will abide forever. Oh, Fathers, Mothers, give him as a gift to your dear ones, and that gift will be theirs always.

Often children are thought to be too young for Bible truths, and other methods are employed to pave the way for that learning, while all the time a child's mind is ready to be indelibly impressed with the gentle goodness of Jesus. They can come to love and serve him very early, indeed, for they are hungry to learn and if given a chance, will do so eagerly.

Little five-year-old Pat, whose parents were too busy socially to attend to any religious education of their son but who haphazardly allowed him to attend church school, was truly eager for knowledge. One Sunday the teacher was doing her best to lead up to the deeper truths, and she brought out pictures of birds and butterflies to show to the children. Young Pat stood up, arms akimbo, and said firmly, if ungrammatically, "I come here to learn about Jesus and the devil, and I don't want to see no butterflies." There was a child hungering for the truth and who felt that time was surely being wasted.

Children are never too young to be told of Jesus and his love. First impressions are lasting, and parents who are conscious of this fact will waste no time in introducing even the littlest ones to Jesus. We are told to "train up a child in the way he should go: and when he is old, he will not depart from it." Oh, Fathers, Mothers, from their cradle days give your children to Christ. Remember that when he was on the earth, he said: "Suffer the little children to come unto me, and forbid them not: for of such is the kingdom of God."

In family life there should be dignity. Each individual's rights should be respected from the youngest to the oldest. Each child differs from the others. That difference must be sought out and considered in daily family living. Children should be taught the command: "Honour thy father and thy mother"; but quite as important, the parents must prove themselves worthy of that honor, or there can be none of it.

A beautiful and talented young mother was leading the devotions before an interested group. She stood up, Bible in hand. "I am going to tell a story," she began, "about a modern mother. This mother was what might be termed a 'perfectionist.' Her house was always immaculate, her children were well dressed, her husband was kind and good, but evidently he sensed that everything about the house must be kept orderly if things were to run smoothly and as a result was often uncomfortable.

"This mother did a great deal of church work. She was a devotional leader, a worker with the P.T.A., a busy clubwoman, and she did all these outside tasks in a consciously charming and gracious manner. Many friends expressed admiration for her unusual ability, they praised her highly, and they 'just did not see how she managed to do everything so well, so beautifully.' And," continued the speaker, "the woman literally basked in that praise. In fact she simply ate it up and craved more. It did a great deal for her ego.

"Then suddenly she realized that at home there was something lacking. There she heard no flattering comment. She did not seem to have the honor and the glory she received elsewhere. She was hurt and indignant over it for a while, and then she began thinking things out. Her husband certainly was changed. There seemed to be nothing in common between them any more. Her children were eager to escape to a neighbor's house or to be anywhere but at home. She realized that she herself was not the sweet charming person she was out in public. She found that she grew irritable over any disorder in the home. She had become overly critical of those she loved most on earth, and, well, something was wrong. She was miserable and frightened.

"One day while studying her Bible for the next meeting, she came upon the thirteenth chapter of First Corinthians: 'If I speak with the tongues of men and of angels, but have not love, I am become sounding brass, or a clanging cymbal.' She stopped, amazed. 'That's exactly what is happening to me,' she said to herself, 'and my words are nothing but brass!' She read on: 'Love suffereth long, and is kind; love envieth not; love vaunteth not itself, is not puffed up, doth not behave itself unseemly, seeketh not its own, is not provoked. . . . Love never faileth.' Here was the crux of the matter. Had she not been vaunting herself? Surely she had been 'puffed up.' She had been provoked at home too easily, her love had often failed; she had not suffered long and been ever kind. She was no longer lovable to herself, and something had to be done and done at once.

"That something was not accomplished at once, but with God's help she changed her own mode of living, and in so doing she changed the family life completely. She started family devotions that had been sadly neglected. She put first things first in her household, and sensing the change, her husband became his old loving and lovable self. The children were happy to stay at home, where a miracle had taken place, and peace reigned."

The speaker stood for a moment, the sunlight shining through a window upon her beautiful, earnest face. There was no pretense or vanity here. Then she spoke again: "We are told that honest confession is good for the soul. May it be so. That was a true story, and I am that woman."

Oh, the responsibility of parents! Church school cannot do the task. The day school often fails in its responsibility. The job belongs to the parents also. When the great work of rearing children for the Lord is accomplished, home is the dearest, the most sacred place in the world. The community is bettered as youth go forth from the home ready to take their places in the world, and the nation becomes stronger, greater, more able to cope with the great forces of the earth, because youth has been trained to go forth, able to serve mankind, and to battle for the right.

Dear heavenly Father, as parents we need thy constant guidance. Thou hast given us a great responsibility—so great that only through thy help can we rear our children as thou wouldst have us do. May we be good examples. Give us thy wisdom and thy strength that we may do this great work well. Amen.

I Have Called You Friends

————————————————————

Greater love hath no man than this, that a man lay down his life for his friends. Ye are my friends, if ye do whatsoever I command you. Henceforth I call you not servants; for the servant knoweth not what his lord doeth: but I have called you friends; for all things that I have heard of my Father I have made known unto you.

—John 15:13-15

HERE IS the greatest, the tenderest, and the most beautiful tribute man has ever had paid him. Christ was speaking directly to his disciples of that day, but he was also addressing you, he was addressing me. He was speaking to any of his followers down the ages who keep his commandments and who do his will. All true Christians are striving earnestly to heed his voice and to obey it. We can gladly appropriate Christ's remarkable statement to ourselves.

"I have called you friends!" The Christ who is so far above us—the wonder is that he can even see us. The Christ who is so faultless—we marvel that he can be charitable to us with all our faults and frailties. The Christ who walks and talks with God himself is willing to walk and talk with us. Think of it!

But that is what true friendship is. Webster defines it thus: "Friendship, a close association one with another; a mutual love; an attachment by esteem, respect, and affection." All this and the white Christ calls us his friends! What honor and what glory he has bestowed upon us! May we prove worthy of that singular trust.

Far too often we take our friends for granted. We also many times take our Lord for granted, when hourly our hearts should be singing his praise. We take those whom we love as a matter of course, when we should be alert to express to them our sincere appreciation and affection.

Often our friends have no idea the important part they play in our lives. It would cheer and bless them greatly if they only knew. We are either too shy or too careless to become vocal on this matter of friendship. What a sweetener of life, what encouragement it would be if we would take the time and the trouble to tell the ones walking by our side of our love, and to say it often enough to impress that fact indelibly upon their hearts.

Is it wise to wait until our friends pass on to bring the flowers they would so love could they see and breathe and touch them? Rather should

we not fetch them our "flowers for the living"?
—flowers in the vivid coloring of love and faith,
and heavy with the sweet odor of trust? We need
not purchase those flowers of a florist at great expense. They grow in the garden of our hearts,
and they cost nothing but a brief word or two,
an act of kindliness, an understanding hand-
clasp—inexpensive, indeed, but the recompense
would be beyond price. Surely Christ in his love
for us, his concrete example, expressive of that
love through his many mercies, should be our
shining example. His love never fails. It will be
undeviating throughout eternity. Nothing can
separate us from the love of God.

In our dealings with our friends may we not
take on something of the outgiving spirit of the
Christ? Should we not be true as he is true? Helpful as he is helpful? Understanding as he is understanding? Loyal as he is loyal? With this for
our aim our friendships here would surely be
made in heaven.

It takes so very little, Lord,
  To make a hurt heart glad;
A bit of praise, a loving word,
  Can cheer one who is sad.
Should we withhold the sincere praise
  And go unmindful of

Some kindly overture of one
    Who craves our praise, our love?

The friends who walk the way with us
    So often need our care.
May we reach out a hand to help
    Them with the load they bear.
Like thee, O Lord, we would be kind
    From dawn to day's far end,
Humbly grateful to thee, Lord,
    For thy good gift—a friend.

God grant no friend of ours may ever have occasion, as did Job, to lament: "My familiar friends have forgotten me"—brief, sorrowful words, holding within them the great sadness of loneliness. Paul utters something of the same plaint when he says of a friend: "Demus hath forsaken me." The pity of it rends our hearts.

When we think of heroes, these are truly the greatest, the most outstanding—those who lay down their lives for their friends. We read of it almost daily. We hear of it over our radios, this stark heroism. A boy dives into deep water to save a young friend and drowns. A woman perishes while attempting to rescue a neighbor's baby from a burning building. A man is crushed beneath car wheels while trying to save another from their onrush. Christlike? Yes. He died for us all. He was, and is, our eternal friend.

Our Friend, we thank thee that thou hast honored us by the name of "friends." To be a friend we must prove ourselves worthy. Help us, dear Lord, to do so.

We would study thy ways that we may emulate thee, that our friends in beholding us walking by their side may turn and see thee walking there. Lord, bless all friendships that are worthy of the name. Amen.

19

The Lifted Hands

But Moses' hands were heavy; and they took a stone, and put it under him, and he sat thereon; and Aaron and Hur stayed up his hands, the one on the one side, and the other on the other side; and his hands were steady until the going down of the sun.—Exod. 17:12

THE LEADERS of our day, if their hands are pointing heavenward in a just and righteous cause, should have all the help we can possibly give them to keep those hands steady and lifted high at their tasks.

We must not expect them to have strength beyond human endurance. We must be ready to steady them when they falter and to lend them our strength in their need.

The picture of Moses is very vivid. We see him standing upright upon the hill, patiently and faithfully performing his appointed duty. His was indeed a grave responsibility. Israel prevailed against the enemy only when his hands were lifted. "When he let down his hand Amalek prevailed."

Doubtless through most of the morning his upward thrust hands expressed unlimited endurance and courage, but Moses' sinews and bones were made of human stuff even as are ours, and he began to falter and to fail in the heat of the day, as we so often do.

His associates made him as comfortable as possible, although the seat they brought for him was nothing but a rock.

They saw that his hands were beginning to waver and then fall listlessly at his side, and they knew his strength was utterly spent. They then conceived the idea of holding up his hands themselves, and thus they helped him bear on until the "going down of the sun."

How often we, too, wait until those who are serving us are worn to the point of exhaustion. Should we not stand beside them, ever ready to strengthen their hands and encourage their hearts before their strength fails?

Our missionaries are waging the greatest battles of all time. Their work is made more difficult because of the great and terrible forces that are fighting God and thus fighting them. They are too often all but forgotten by those of us at home. There are days when we forget to pray for them and fail to send the needed funds to help carry on their great work. We should be standing by to aid them in every way possible.

They bear on through the heat of the day, then often they falter beneath burdens too heavy for their endurance. They either go on until their life forces are spent, or they are forced to return home with their work half done—a work so greatly needed. Perhaps had we been more faithful, they could have finished that work.

"Strengthen ye the weak hands, and confirm the feeble knees. Say to them that are of a fearful heart, Be strong, fear not: behold, your God will come with vengeance, even God with a recompence; he will come and save you."

We have our orders from above. We have the words that we should speak, put into our mouths to cheer and bless and encourage the worn and weary laborers for the Lord, who grow tired in the heat of the day. Shall we not heed those orders? Shall we not make good use of the words?

We here in our own land are groping in a strange darkness. We need a hand that holds a lifted lamp. There are things we can do to help. Let us ever be watchful to serve when service is needed. Prayer can work wonders. Should we not pray more?

The ministers in our churches need the layman's prayers. They need their lifted hands held steady. Our church-school teachers often grow discouraged. They should have our understanding, our sympathy, and our encouragement. Shall

we not be more mindful of all who serve through
the days in countless different ways?

If we hold firmly onto those lifted hands, if we
stay them as we should, the battles we are fighting today will be won. If we neglect to do so,
God alone knows what will be the result.

A ship was coming slowly into New York
harbor. A child stood beside his mother at the
rail watching with wonder the Statue of Liberty,
which caught and held the evening sun on her
high-lifted arm. Suddenly he turned to his mother
and said, "Mother, I should think her arm would
get tired. Doesn't she need someone to help
her hold up the light?"

The wise mother answered, "Yes, dear, she
does need someone—you, me, all of us—to hold
up that particular light; and her arm would have
grown tired long ago had it not been for the
lifting love for our land that is in the hearts of
all true Americans."

Truly the great humanitarian mother who lifts
her lamp beside our open door needs every man,
woman, and child in our midst today to help
her hold the light above the land and sea. Oh,
that others seeing that light may find in it something pure and holy and precious, a light for
all the world to steer their courses by.

God grant we may undergird this symbol of
our faith in God and goodness by our prayers,

with our hands ready for service and with a strong clear faith. Only thus can we steady the arm and help hold up the light.

Our gracious Lord, we would be stayers of the hands that are lifted to serve us. We would help hold the light of thy truth and righteousness high that all the lost of earth may find their way out of darkness into the light. We pray for thy strength and thy wisdom as we take our way. Grant it to us we pray, for we ask it in Jesus' name. Amen.

20

Immortality

God . . . hath saved us, and called us with an holy calling, not according to our works, but according to his own purpose and grace, which was given us in Christ Jesus before the world began, but is now made manifest by the appearing of our Saviour Jesus Christ, who hath abolished death, and hath brought life and immortality to light through the gospel.—II Tim. 1:9-10

WHAT PRAISE, what thanksgiving could adequately express mankind's gratitude to the Lord Jesus Christ for his marvelous act of bringing "life" and "immortality" to light through his Word?

The darkness must have truly been dense over the earth before his coming. Hitherto the light had not fully been revealed. Men went groping in uncertainty. Death was a thing to fear. Such words as these came sounding mournfully down the years: "Forgotten as a dead man." "The dead praise not the Lord," "The dead know not any thing"—heart-breaking statements with no comfort in them whatsoever for the bereaved or for those about to pass from this world.

But Jesus' coming, his death, his resurrection, shed a light like that of high noon over the world to cheer and bless humanity in its dire need for assurance, for certainty in the dark through which it was going. He gave the blessed word. "I am the resurrection, and the life," and this: "He that believeth in me, though he were dead, yet shall he live."

Within these statements lies all the hope of mankind. Our simple part is to believe. He will do the rest.

We look about us. We see the tiny acorn taking root, lifting up to become a great tree. Some force is drawing it upward from the dark caverns of the earth. The force that performed that miracle of life over death can, without question, perform for us.

We note a beautiful life, a follower of the Christ, a vivid personality, one made in the image of God himself; and we know for a certainty that our Lord, who abhors waste, would never allow for a moment the loss of this vital living soul.

We are often questioners. We want proof. We want to know what sort of place it is to which we are going. Faith and trust can be the answer. We can believe that these bodies of ours will resemble the body which Christ wore after his resurrection—bodies freed from the burdens of an earthly lifetime. We are made in his image. We shall be like him. This is enough and all we need to know.

There is the story told of a young girl who longed to know the truth and meaning of immortality. One day she went to her pastor's study and found him ready to receive her. As she left his office, she felt that the good doctor had been very vague and unsatisfactory. He had not really given her one valid argument for the belief in the persistence of personality over death. He had spoken of the immortality of the soul and had made the words sound wonderful, but she thought: "That is purely emotional." College had taught her that emotion was never a proof of anything.

"My dear child," he had said, "there are only two things that can give you the assurance of the immortality of the soul—a close friendship with Jesus Christ or some deep personal experience that makes you realize his love. You cannot find proof of it in a textbook any more than you can find proof of any of the great realities of life: of truth, justice, courage—of love itself. You cannot weigh them on any scale or test them in the laboratory. The proof that they are lies in

the things that they make people do. It is so
with immortality."

His talk made the girl vaguely uncomfortable,
but she shrugged away the discomfort, telling
herself that the doctor was too old to have anything to give to the youth of today.

She was a secretary, often on call, and when
she opened her door, the telephone was ringing.
A friend was calling. "Could you come over
for a few minutes?" she questioned. The girl was
pleased and flattered, for the woman was a leader
in many civic movements. She had worked with
her before and had admired her executive ability.
She was a bit excited as she reached the big
house. A maid directed her to the room where
her friend sat in an easy chair before the fire.

"I wonder if I can ask you to help me in
something that may be a bit hard for you,"
said the woman.

"I will gladly if you can trust me," came the
answer.

The woman smiled. "You are such an ideal
secretary—I can trust you. I have a journey
to make, and I want to leave everything in order so that no one will have to be bothered by
loose ends."

"Oh, you are going abroad!" the girl cried
excitedly. "Whatever shall we do without you?
I am so glad for you." Her sentence broke, and

she suddenly went white. A terrible thought had occurred to her. Surely her friend could not mean that!

The older woman's eyes met hers with a quiet smile. "Yes, my dear, I mean the great journey. Isn't it good of God to let me know so that I can leave things in order? The doctor gives me a month. Will you help me?"

Later the girl left the house. There were tears in her eyes, a lump in her throat, but her head was high. She had found the answer. The unfaltering faith of her friend was like a testament signed by the hand of God himself. Suddenly the minister's words came clearly, they did not seem so impossible now.

Oh, love that will not let us go! Even after death that love holds more surely, more closely, than here where our proneness to wander makes our contact with our Lord grow slack at times through our own faults and failures.

Often the dying saints of earth have been firm witnesses for the proof of life after death. Even in their passing we have seen them waken to sudden consciousness, their eyes alight, their faces radiant with the reflected glory from the heavenly city. There is no doubt. Life after death is as certain as the Word of God which will never pass away.

Lord God, help us as earthly pilgrims to keep
the certainty of immortality ever before our eyes.
There are few of us hardy enough or strong enough
to doubt this truth without grave spiritual harm.
We know, because thou hast said so, that there
are heavenly mansions awaiting all those who believe in thee. Let us not be troubled. We do believe, and we thank thee and praise thee for the
blessed assurance of a heavenly home that thou
hast prepared for us.

Keep our vision clear that we may look forward
with joy to an eternity with thee. Amen.

21

The Unsearchable Riches

O Lord, how manifold are thy works! In wisdom hast thou made them all: the earth is full of thy riches.—Ps. 104:24

And I will give thee the treasures of darkness, and hidden riches of secret places, that thou mayest know that I, the Lord, which call thee by thy name, am the God of Israel.—Isa. 45:3

"The unsearchable riches"—here in this one
      book
   Is all of life, all of eternity.
One searching for great treasures need not look
   Further than this—further than here to see
The entrance and the depth of that great mine
Where all God's buried golden nuggets shine.

Here in the breadth and depth and length and
      height
   Of God's Word lie the treasures all may take.

An understanding heart can bring to light
   The gold that has been stored there for our
      sake:
A vein that never can be fully mined
By all the avid seeking of mankind.

Oh, let us dig as miners dig for gold,
For the unsearchable riches that these pages hold.

OFTEN WE come upon some strangely revealing phrase in our Bible reading, words that stand out as luminously as pearls with their gleaming high lights, their delicate shadows. We may be reading, and suddenly the eye, the mind, the heart, are all arrested with a thought so vital, so clearly expressed, so definitely for our good, that it is as if a voice had spoken to us aloud.

Here is one such phrasing; not in its beauty is it arresting, but because of the intense meaning of the words and the stark fact of a man's turning to his God for help in his day of trouble. "And David was greatly distressed; for the people spake of stoning him, because the soul of all the people was grieved, every man for his sons and for his daughters; but David encouraged himself in the Lord his God." (I Sam. 30:6.) This is a thought most worthy of consideration. If David encouraged himself in the Lord, should not we do likewise when we are troubled? Is it not a helpful thought that this can be done?

The Ziklag country had been pillaged, and wives, sons, and daughters were taken captive. History often repeats itself, and the human heart is the same the world over. Trouble is trouble in any land. The implements become more deadly with the passing of time, and evil is evil in any language. To have one's loved ones taken captive by an enemy would do the same thing to the souls of men today. We are told that "David and the people that were with him lifted up their voice and wept, until they had no more power to weep."

We know of stricken lands today. Hunger stalks the people in such lands as India and Korea. In many cases their homes are gone, families have been brutally separated; they sit with dry eyes and inert hands because there are no more tears to be shed and there is nothing more to be done. The agony on their faces expresses that grief as clearly as weeping could do. Without doubt those who may have found the Lord to be their friend do as David did of old—they encourage themselves in the Lord their God.

What is there left for the heart to do in such stress and agony? Where can we turn for help save to the Lord our God? We read on, and we find that David "enquired at the Lord," and the Lord gave him the encouragement he so much needed. He told him to go and overtake the enemy. He said: "Pursue: for thou shalt surely overtake them, and without fail recover all"; and it came to pass as the Lord had said. His Word is ever unfailing, and David was heartened to go on with his monumental task.

We recall that as he and his four hundred men who were strong went in hurried pursuit, they came upon an Egyptian who had been abandoned by his master "Because three days agone I fell sick"; and he went on to say, "We made an invasion upon the south of the Chere-thites, . . . and we burned Ziklag with fire." History repeating itself!

But David was in the right; God stood by him, and his loved ones were restored to him. He was strengthened for his task because of the hope the Lord had put into his heart in answer to his prayer. He had "encouraged himself in the Lord."

How many examples we have in the blessed Word of God that we can follow! Through utter darkness a light can shine; through every stress there can be hope. The power is still there, unfailing, waiting to be used. We press a button, and we flood our homes with light. We pray, and if we pray aright—which is according to

the will of God—our souls are suddenly filled
with the light of hope. Our doubts are dispelled,
and we can go forward able to face our days simply
because we have encouraged ourselves in the
Lord our God.

Truly in the most prosaic statements in our
Bible we can come upon the great unsearchable
riches that the Lord has put there for us to find.

Our dear heavenly Father, we are grateful to
thee for meeting our every need through thy Word.
We need only to search for thy help, and we can
find it between the covers of one book—thy book,
set for our guidance through time and eternity.
Help us to search for thy riches. Help us to encourage ourselves in thee, that we may be more
than conquerors on the way we go. Amen.

22

The Importuning Voice

O earth, earth, earth, hear the word of the Lord.
—Jer. 22:29

THE CRY sounds down the ages, insistent and persistent, within it something of the pathos and heartbreak of Christ's lament over Jerusalem: "O Jerusalem, . . . how often would I have gathered thy children together, even as a hen gathered her chickens under her wings, and ye would not!"

Strange that early and late the children of earth must be petitioned to hear the warning cry which, if heeded, would mean their soul's salvation, their everlasting good. One wonders at the perversity of the human race.

In Christ's lament over Jerusalem there are patience and sorrow combined, but in the words of Isaiah (34:1) there is righteous indignation: "Come near, ye nations, to hear; and hearken, ye people: let the earth hear, and all that is therein; the world, and all things that come forth of it." Here is definite warning that all lands should be quick to hear and heed today lest judgment come upon us.

Again in Isaiah we hear the cry: "Ho, every one that thirsteth, come ye to the waters. . . . Hearken diligently unto me. . . . Incline your ear, and come unto me; hear, and your soul shall live." The word "hear" is the keynote of countless commands throughout the Word of God. It is the eternal plea of a great and just Father to his children.

David, the psalmist, makes answer: "I will hear what God the Lord will speak: for he will speak peace unto his people, and to his saints." Then comes the warning, definite and clear: "But let them not turn again to folly." Is it not a just and righteous God speaking through the psalmist to us today?

In searching for the truth we come upon these hopeful, helpful words: "When thou art in tribulation, and all these things are come upon thee, even in the latter days, if thou turn to the Lord thy God, and shalt be obedient unto his voice; (For the Lord thy God is a merciful God;) he will not forsake thee, neither destroy thee, nor forget the covenant of thy fathers which he sware unto them." (Deut. 4:30-31.)

The small word "if" is meaningful and vastly important all through the Word of God: "If thou turn to the Lord thy God." "If my people,

which are called by my name, shall . . . turn
from their wicked ways; . . . I . . . will heal their
land." It is only if conditions are met will it
be well with us in the land of the living. It is
plain that if our nation today is not to perish,
we must turn from our evil ways and follow after
righteousness. God says so, and God does not lie.

There is no doubt but that we are in the
"latter days." Shall we not be quick and obedient
to follow our Lord's commands? How it must
hurt his great loving heart to call and not be
answered! We recall the parable of the king who
made a marriage feast for his son. It is briefly
stated: he sent out the word, "and they would
not come."

It calls to mind an incident that holds something of the hurt the king must have felt to have
his invitations slighted. It happened to a humble
woman of our modern times. She was a good
woman at heart, kind and generous to a fault; but
she had had no opportunity to learn how to
"measure up" to modern society. Her speech
was uncouth, her taste in dress, bad. Her ap-
pearance was decidedly against her.

However, she had a young daughter who was
seemingly popular with her schoolmates and
who, strangely enough, was inately refined. She
loved her mother, and nothing would ever in-
duce her to hurt that mother, although she often

sensed the difference between her and the other girls' mothers; and she was troubled by the comparison.

As the girl's birthday neared, her mother suggested a birthday party to which the girl's classmates and their mothers were to be invited. Great preparations took place. The shabby little below-the-tracks house shone with cleanliness; the food was prepared. Finally the hour came. The mother was dressed in her overly fussy dress, the daughter in her more sedate clothing. The great moment had arrived, and they sat waiting. The guests were late.

"The clock surely must be wrong."

"Go peep through the curtains—they must be coming now."

"Look again!"

But the guests were not there—they did not come at all. The slight was all too evident; the hurt caused was pitifully acute.

How awful a thing it is to hurt our heavenly Father, when we refuse to accept his invitation to "come." How miserably thoughtless and unkind we are at times to our fellow men! Shall we not, indeed, turn from our evil ways and hear and heed the calls that come to us—calls that if obeyed, will make for finer, better Christian living?

"O earth, earth, earth, hear the word of the Lord."

Our heavenly Father, too often we have been heedless in our dealings with thee and with our kind. Forgive us, we pray. Unstop our deaf ears, and open our minds for us, that we may hear thy voice and follow its dictations. Only thus, we know, will we as individuals be blest and as a nation be saved. We would be eager and willing to do thy will and to help make thy kingdom come upon the earth. Amen.

23

As Thy Servant Was Busy

As thy servant was busy here and there, he was gone.—I Kings 20:40

"BUSY HERE and there."—is this not a true picture of many a professing Christian today? "Busy here"—making money, climbing socially, grasping for fame and power. "Busy there"— doing over a thousand inconsequential things, often harmful in themselves. Any thoughtful person can name them. One of the things we are busiest over is the idling away of the hours that are meted out to us by the time clock of eternity—time that passes and can never be reclaimed.

As we are thus busy, how many tasks set us by the hand of God, needing much to be done, are ignored and neglected? Further on in the above scripture we see the outcome of this neglect, as the king replies: "So shall thy judgment be; thyself hast decided it." Unknowingly we pass judgment on ourselves as we decide our fate.

On the other hand, if we set ourselves to follow the Lord's instructions, we are awarded with life—beautiful, productive, joyous life. If we fail in our set duties, the result is nothing short of death. This can be avoided only if there is a definite change in our mode of living before it is too late.

"What doth the Lord thy God require of thee, but to fear the Lord thy God, to walk in all his ways, and to love him, and to serve the Lord thy God with all thy heart and with all thy soul, to keep the commandments of the Lord." (Deut. 10:12-13.)

We here have it summed up simply for us that we may have no excuse of not understanding. We are to fear the Lord. This does not mean that we come shrinkingly and tremblingly before him, but it means reverence and love for him on our part. We are to walk in his way, and having the way clearly marked out for us, we need not lose that way. We are to love him for his great love for us. We are to walk humbly; we are to keep his commandments; we are to help others. We are to be busy at this, our appointed task.

We may be sure that the Lord wants his children to have clean and wholesome recreation. He wants us to mingle happily and helpfully with our kind. He must love much the sound of joyous laughter rising to him from the earth.

But we also may be sure that he demands to be first in our lives.

What does the Lord require of you? What does he require of me? We have it held before our eyes like a clearly painted chart. Let us truly get busy.

We can be very busy at being "kind one to another, tenderhearted, forgiving one another," as Christ has often forgiven us. We can be fully occupied in growing in grace. A dear Christian woman who had been very ill and was unexpectedly restored to health was questioning the why of her survival, and she humbly came to the conclusion that she had been spared to "grow in grace." God must have been pleased at her gentle acceptance of the gracious task she had set for herself. He must be very proud of any of his children who set themselves to do his will.

We can be busy, indeed, in cultivating faith. We can through greater and fuller trust burnish that stuff we know as "the substance of things hoped for," until it gleams in our breasts like rubbed silver. How often have any of us made a thorough investigating journey through our beings? The intelligence God planted in man, when he became a living soul, should surely grow like a virgin forest through the years.

There are trails to be blazed in the realms of thought which will let the sunlight through to shed a clearer light upon the problems and perplexities of our daily living. There are unexplored paths in imagination to be tended until they blossom into the radiant poetry of living. Exploring one's own being for possibilities and capabilities is not introversion in a wrong sense. Rather it is a reaching out and upward in order to discover and develop one's highest service for God and man.

Where there are faults and failures, there should be the immediate surgery of God's forgiveness and healing. Where strange and beautiful discoveries are made, these new riches should be shared by others. Every day we should forge further into the waiting continents of our being. Each hour we should draw nearer the higher altitudes of vigorous life and service. Unless we know ourselves, how can we teach others to find their own vast reaches, their own great possibilities? God helping us, if we are thus busy, we may find ourselves better and greater than we know.

The fields, Christ said, are white unto harvest. He said it long ago. How much whiter are they now after all these centuries? Should we not be busy in those fields for the Master? We should learn to be helpful in one place at a time, not "here and there," scattering our resources and our energies, and accomplishing nothing. We should be busy in the Lord's way.

Within the human heart are many regions,
    Undreamed of and still waiting to be found.
There are new paths to blaze in thought and
        action,
    Far journeys to be made to higher ground.
In the undiscovered countries of our being
    Are forces steeped with power; there is new,
Wide knowledge to be gained through toil and
        study;
    There is startling creative work to do.

So many strange resources to discover:
    God's given graces that have gone unnamed,
High courage for some unexpected testing,
    Prayer power that has not yet been fully
        claimed.
So many regions in us undiscovered,
    Such possibilities within each breast!
The wealth of unmined jewels, heights un-
        conquered,
    Await the seeker in this glorious quest.

Our Father and our God, where we have failed
thee, and thou knowest that we have done so often,
forgive us, we pray. Help us to realize the importance of time in our lives, the value of the moments. We would be useful to thee. We would
live up to thy requirements. Guide us as we strive
to be busy in thy behalf, that we may bear fruit
for time and for eternity. We ask it in thy Son's
dear name. Amen.

24

Abide With Us

And they drew nigh unto the village, whither they went: and he made as though he would have gone further. But they constrained him, saying, Abide with us: for it is toward evening, and the day is far spent. And he went in to tarry with them.
—Luke 24:28-29

Upon the far Emmaus road,
  Behold, two of them went their way;
Amazed, distressed, uncomforted,
  They trod the road that day.
Then One came walking by their side,
  A stranger to their holden eyes.
"How is it that thou dost commune
  In this sad wonder-wise?"
He questioned, and one made reply:
  "Thou art a stranger." Then he saith,
"Else thou wouldst know concerning one,
  Jesus of Nazareth,
Who was a prophet great indeed,
  But now condemned and crucified;
And three long days it hath been since
  Our blessed Lord hath died.

129

Now women coming to the tomb
  Before the early morning dawn
Have spoken thus, 'An angel stood,
  But our dear Lord was gone!'
Wistful we were and trusted much
  That Israel should be redeemed
By this same Jesus, but alas,
  It were as if we dreamed."

.   .   .   .

Ah, we so slow of heart to know
  'Tis Jesus walking by our side.
Constrain him for 'tis evening time—
  With us, O Lord, abide.
With us abide, the day is spent;
  Footsore and weary we would rest;
Come tarry with us, stay with us,
  Our King, our Lord, our Guest.

VOLUMES have been written and sung and
said of the glory of the Easter morning, and well it
is that men have been caught up in awe and
reverence before those early hours when the
greatest event in history took place: the garden,
the dawn, the sunburst, the joy and the wonder
over the resurrection of our blessed Lord—so
fraught with meaning for us all that it outshines
every other earthly happening.

There has not been so much thought given
to one of the tenderest episodes in the Word of

God—that of the evening hour in a little humble home in Emmaus. We are indebted to Luke for the narrative, and we should be inordinately grateful to him for relating the beautiful incident.

The night was coming down as Cleopas and Simon, with the stranger by their side, drew near to the little village of Emmaus. Doubtless they were tired after their long walk from Jerusalem and were pleased at last to see the early-lighted lamps of the little town, glimmering like so many fireflies through the dusk.

The shadows deepened on the near-by field and darkened the roofs and streets of the little town. And then Cleopas' home was just around the corner. As they drew nearer to it, the stranger spoke of going on farther; but they would have none of it. Here was a courteous person whom they instinctively liked. He would not be one to go into any man's house uninvited. At their insistence he accepted their urgent invitation to tarry with them for a while.

The evening meal was in the process of being cooked. Sundown of the Jewish Sabbath lifted the ban from the laborless day, and the goodwife had gone about her usual household tasks. The odor of food came pleasantly to their nostrils. They were expected, and the housemother was getting the men a good supper.

We can see them entering the door. The low

lintel caused the tall stranger to stoop a bit as he passed inside. He was a gracious guest, and he was received graciously. Their sandals were removed, the basins were brought out for the washing of their feet, and then supper was served.

The stranger sat at the table with them. He took the proffered bread; he blessed it; he broke it and gave thanks above it. He handed it out to them, and suddenly, like a revealing flash of lightning, they recognized their Lord—the Christ who had been crucified and buried three days ago. Oh, the wonder of it! The rapture, the surprise, the joy, in that humble household that night!

It is not strange that they hurried back to Jerusalem! No longer were they tired and heavy-hearted; no longer were they bereft. They hastened to break the good news to the waiting ones in Jerusalem. The Christ was back among them again—the Christ who had been the light, the hope, and the purpose of their days; the Christ whom they loved so devotedly, so passionately. Their praises rang out on the night air like so many clear-struck bells.

Here is a strange and beautiful truth: today, after the long centuries, that same Jesus will enter into the humblest home in any land to abide there. If he is invited to do so, he will tarry in our midst, an invisible and permanent presence, to sit at our table with us, to break bread with us, and will reveal himself to us if we but make him welcome.

The family that is conscious of that presence, becomes a better family by far because he is there. The members become alert to please their guest. There is courtesy where there might be rudeness, kindness where unkindness would be evident, gentleness where harshness and intolerance might enter in. He shares the roof, the fire, the food; for he is ever a living force in our midst. He will walk with us and talk with us, and strengthen and guide and comfort us.

With this indwelling Christ in the home such a home becomes the bulwark of a nation. So long as there are Christian homes, there is hope for any land, even though that land is stricken sore. The hope of any nation's survival lies in that type of home and in the Christ-trained youth that go out from that home—youth who put Christ first in their daily living, who find him ever an invisible support.

"Abide with us," for it is toward the evening. Truly the coming night may be nearer for many of us than we think. He has walked and talked with us on the long journey through the heat of the day; we must not permit the one who has companioned us so graciously to go farther. Let us be insistent in our pleading: "Abide with us."

Our roof is thine; our table is spread for thee.
Break bread with us and bless us, for truly without thee we are undone.

Our gracious Guest, we pray thee "abide with
us." Come enter our door. Be the head of our
household, our companion and our counselor.
We need thee every hour. Make us conscious of
thy abiding presence that we may do nothing, say
nothing, that will dishonor thee. Amen.

25

Adventure in Christian Reading

Only take heed to thyself, and keep thy soul diligently, lest thou forget the things which thine eyes have seen, and lest they depart from thy heart all the days of thy life: but teach them thy sons, and thy sons' sons.—Deut. 4:9

O PARENTS, heed the command today. Teach your children early the might and the power and the beauty of God's Word. Let them dream dreams, and see visions, whose sources can be found in the most exquisite literature of all time —our Bible.

Too much cheapness has been the food of our young. Teach them, help them to find the beauty and truth in the library of our Lord. They are craving adventure perhaps—give it to them. Adventure is associated with some remarkable experience, an issue hanging upon unforeseen events, or with romance of vivid and picturesque language that lifts one from the commonplace of everyday living into mystic lands of splendor and delight.

Let them find it; it is daily at their fingertips if they but seek for it. The humblest of us can possess the greatest library, which consists of sixty-six classics. There is no more vital and vivid literature in all the world than that which, under one cover, is known as the Bible.

There love and passion, beauty and truth, abound. There is action, on which so many today seem to depend for entertainment—action of red-blooded men who were chosen of God to battle for the right. There are conflicts, which are ever demanded of writers whether it is truth or fiction they are penning.

Where could be found a more touching love story than that of Isaac and Rebecca? Or where a more tender romance than the courtship of Jacob for Rachel? Surely in their case there was conflict enough to satisfy any demanding reader.

The story of Joseph is sheer high adventure, while the book of Ruth is a love epic of faith and loyalty that has never been surpassed. Esther in her passion for her own race fires the heart with admiration, while Job thrills us with his steadfastness of purpose despite the calamities that befell him. On and on we might go through the Old Testament, seeking for and finding heroes and heroines that make for exciting, satisfying, and adventurous reading; but it is in the "New Testament of our Lord and Savior Jesus

Christ," that the most amazing, heart-warming, heart-rending books of this priceless library can be found.

Here we come upon the supreme adventure of one man's birth, life, and death. It has changed the channel of billions of souls. Never after the first Christmas Eve of long ago could this old earth be the same. Because of God's almost incomprehensible sacrifice we are a changed people. Think of it! God had had the companionship of this marvelous Son for countless ages. They had been together "in the glory that was before the world began!"

Think of them often—Father and Son, standing together, watching the breath-taking splendor of splintering light as the sun and moon and stars whirled off into space and took shape. They stood planning the world as an Eden. They were to make man in their own image. Then, because those same men failed them, because they sinned and then were in desperate need, the Father sent his Son to live and die for us! How he must love us!

There could be no greater adventure than that of Christ's lifetime achievement. From the moment of his birth, when the sky was rent with joyous heralding and his special star rode the heavens to guide to his feet the humble men of the fields as well as the kings of earth, up to his last hour on the spring hillside, when he took his way back to the waiting Father, there is reading that shakes the soul with electrifying intensity.

We go further into research in our library, and we find Stephen, the young martyr, giving up his life for this same Christ. We come upon Saul of Tarsus, consenting to his death because he believed he was doing God's service. And then the light! and his eyes were opened to the living Saviour. What glorious service he rendered the kingdom from then on!

Age will find itself companioned in the book of Acts, and youth will find its counterpart over and over in the men who stepped boldly out to follow the blessed Lord. It is good reading for us all.

If one is seeking for depth which is seemingly beyond the intelligence of the average reader, let him con the book of Revelation. Here one can ponder for days over a single verse, then like a mirror held to the sunlight the dazzling meaning will break upon the mind and heart until one feels that here, indeed, is an adventurous experience in booklore.

Turn to your *Pilgrim's Progress*—an old, old book, so beautifully written that the modern writer would do well to con it often and long as a guidance in words. It is a book written by one who had suffered much for his convictions. It is a tale of man's eternal search for the highest, his upward climb toward the light. Truly it is

A saga of man's search across the sod
For the everlasting citadels of God.

Take it from the shelf. Dust it off. It will be well worth your while to start with Christian on his celestial journey: the journey we all are to make if we are undeviatingly certain of the road we want to travel. Surely here is adventure in living—from the dark Slough of Despond, on through the Doubting Castle, and later climbing the glittering hills to step onto the shore of eternity.

Thank God for the vast cultural life of today. May we lay hold upon it; may we point out to our children the steppingstones that lead toward finer, cleaner, and better living.

Our heavenly Father, we have so much for which to thank thee, but we have no words with which to praise thee for the privilege we have of thy companionship through thy Word. May we be alert in passing on the good news, not only to our children, but to all who need a guiding light upon their journey to the Holy City. We pray this in Jesus' name. Amen.

26

The Beatitudes

Blessed are the poor in spirit: for theirs is the kingdom of heaven.

Lord, I would be humble,
  Knowing that I am weak.
Often my footsteps falter,
  My tongue is slow to speak.
Spirit divine, I pray thee,
  My intercessor be—
In praying to the Father,
  Pray thou for me.

Blessed are they that mourn: for they shall be comforted.

I would flee from every sorrow
  And seek for joy, instead,
But I know that thou art with me,
  And I am comforted.
Joy is the fruit of sorrow,
  Gladness, the child of pain.

140

Help me to wait the harvest
    That follows the bitter rain.

*Blessed are the meek: for they shall inherit the
earth.*

A quiet, gentle spirit
    Is a boon that I would seek.
Arrogance and false pride
    Are foreign to the meek.
Thy unmerited favor
    Is all I have of worth,
And thy magnificent promise,
    The heritage of the earth.

*Blessed are they which do hunger and thirst after
righteousness: for they shall be filled.*

Lord, I am ever hungry—
    Break thou the bread of life;
My throat is parched and thirsty—
    May each found spring be rife
With clear, cold, living water
    That my clamoring need be stilled.
I praise thee for thy promise:
    "Seek and ye shall be filled."

*Blessed are the merciful: for they shall obtain
mercy.*

I would have great compassion;
    I would have pity, Lord,
And give myself, my substance,
    Not thinking of reward.
And yet, if in so doing,
    Thy mercy I obtain,
I shall be humbly grateful
    For that eternal gain.

*Blessed are the pure in heart: for they shall see
God.*

I open my heart's door to thee;
    I fling its windows wide;
I sweep out the dust and cobwebs;
    Lord, come in and abide.
Only the pure can see thee,
    Keep thou my vision clear.
I would be ever mindful
    That thou art near—so near!

*Blessed are the peacemakers: for they shall be
called the children of God.*

"Peacemaker" means "connecting
    Two into one." Lord God,
I would go forth, a welder
    Upon the old earth's sod,

To join hurt hearts together,
  To bid all warring cease.
Lord, I would be a worker
  For the blessedness of peace.

Blessed are they which are persecuted for right-eousness' sake: for theirs is the kingdom of heaven.

Hard pressed and persecuted,
  The saints have ever been.
As evil gives no quarter,
  The Christ gives none to sin.
Forever there is battle
  Between the two; Lord, make
Me willing, glad to suffer
  For thy dear kingdom's sake.

Blessed are ye, when men shall revile you, and persecute you, and shall say all manner of evil against you falsely, for my sake.

Beneath this heavy burden
  When friends seem far and few,
I, too, would cry: "Forgive them,
  They know not what they do."
I, too, have borne a cross, Lord,
  O blessed holy One;

Help me to pray as thou didst:
  "Thy will, not mine, be done."

But oh, I am so human,
  I have such need of thee;
I plead again, when praying,
  Pray thou for me.